Harvard
Business
Review

ON

MANAGING YOURSELF

THE HARVARD BUSINESS REVIEW PAPERBACK SERIES

The series is designed to bring today's managers and professionals the fundamental information they need to stay competitive in a fast-moving world. From the preeminent thinkers whose work has defined an entire field to the rising stars who will redefine the way we think about business, here are the leading minds and landmark ideas that have established the *Harvard Business Review* as required reading for ambitious businesspeople in organizations around the globe.

Other books in the series:

Other books in the series (continued):

Harvard Business Review

ON

MANAGING YOURSELF

A HARVARD BUSINESS REVIEW PAPERBACK

The *Harvard Business Review* articles in this collection are available as
individual reprints. Discounts apply to quantity purchases. For information and ordering, please contact Customer Service, Harvard Business
School Publishing, Boston, MA 02163. Telephone: (617) 783-7500 or
(800) 988-0886, 8 A.M. to 6 P.M. Eastern Time, Monday through Friday.
Fax: (617) 783-7555, 24 hours a day. E-mail: custserv@hbsp.harvard.edu.

Library of Congress Cataloging-in-Publication Data
Harvard business review on managing yourself.
     p. cm. — (The Harvard business review paperback series)
    Includes index.
    ISBN 1-59139-970-X
    1. Executive ability. 2. Executives—Training of. 3. Industrial
management. 4. Leadership. I. Series: Harvard business review.
II. Series.
HD38.2.H3746 2005
658.4´09—dc22   2005017058
                                                          CIP

Contents

Harvard Business Review

ON

MANAGING YOURSELF

Almost Ready

How Leaders Move Up

DAN CIAMPA

Executive Summary

MOST DESIGNATED CEO SUCCESSORS are talented, hardworking, and smart enough to go all the way—yet fail to land the top job. What they don't realize is, the qualities that helped them in their climb to the number two position aren't enough to boost them to number one.

In addition to running their businesses well, the author explains, would-be CEOs must master the art of forming coalitions and winning support. They must also sharpen their self-awareness and their sensitivity to the needs of bosses and influential peers because they typically receive little performance feedback once they're on track to become CEO. Indeed, the ability to pick up on subtle cues is often an important part of the test.

When succession doesn't go well—or fails altogether—many people pay the price: employees depending on a smooth handoff at the top, investors expecting continuous leadership, and families uprooted when jobs don't pan out. Among those at fault are boards that do not keep a close watch on the succession process, human resource organizations that should have the capacity to help but are not up to the task, and CEOs who do a poor job coaching potential successors.

But the aspiring CEO also bears some responsibility. He can dramatically increase his chances of success by understanding his boss's point of view, knowing his own limitations, and managing what psychologist Gerry Egan has called the "shadow organization"—the political side of a company, characterized by unspoken relationships and alliances—without being labeled "political." Most of all, he must learn to conduct himself with a level of maturity and wisdom that signals he is ready—not almost ready—to be chief executive.

Shortly after being elected U.S. president in 1960, John Kennedy offered Robert McNamara, then president of Ford, the post of treasury secretary. McNamara turned down the offer, saying he wasn't qualified for the job. Then, Kennedy offered him the job of secretary of defense. When McNamara demurred again for the same reason, a frustrated Kennedy exclaimed: "Bob, there is no school to learn to be president, either!"

Leadership at the top is never easy for even the most experienced people. For someone taking on the job of CEO for the first time, mastering the new skills and sorting out the uncertainties that go with the position can be an overwhelming challenge. So it should come as no surprise that the corner suite has a revolving door. The Center for Creative Leadership has estimated that 40% of new CEOs fail in their first 18 months. What's more, the churn rate is on the rise: In a 2002 study, the center found that the number of CEOs leaving their jobs had increased 10% since 2001. As a recent report from the outplacement firm Challenger, Gray & Christmas points out, "The biggest challenge looming over corporate America [is] finding replacement CEOs."

That's a problem for aspiring chief executives. Look at what we know about the experiences of designated CEO successors—talented and hardworking executives who were successful at each stage in their climb to the number two position. Research conducted in the 1990s (by Michael Watkins, of Harvard Business School, and me) showed that, when promoted from within an organization, less than half the people who reached the number two spot expecting to win the CEO title actually ended up in the position. We also saw more organizations going outside their own ranks to hire designated successors—but disturbingly, once hired, only one-quarter of these candidates were successful at either being named CEO or at staying in the CEO job for more than two years.

Clearly, there is an urgent need for CEOs and boards of directors to have an efficient and effective succession process, but few do. While HR departments should be driving the process, most have neither the skills to translate best practices nor the credibility with boards to make an impact. Many corporations—even family-owned businesses, where the financial security of generations is at stake—don't even get as far as having a plan. A 2002 survey by the MassMutual Financial Group and the George and Robin Raymond Family Business Institute showed that although 40% of the polled chairmen and CEOs planned to retire within four years, 55% of the ones age 61 or older had not settled on a succession plan.

But would-be CEOs must also bear responsibility for their success. All too often, they fail to recognize that the qualities they must demonstrate to make the leap from likely successor to CEO are different from the skills they relied on to get to the number two position. In addition to excelling at running their businesses, aspiring CEOs must master the art of forming coalitions and winning the support of people who are competitors. These are elements of what psychologist Gerry Egan has called the "shadow organization"—the political side of a company, characterized by unspoken relationships, alliances, and influence exerted by coalitions. Because, in most cases, aspiring CEOs receive little actionable feedback once they become designated successors, they must sharpen their self-awareness as well as their sensitivity to the wants and needs of bosses and influential peers; they must learn to conduct themselves with a level of maturity and wisdom that signals to boards as well as CEOs that they are ready—not just almost ready—to be chief executive.

The CEO Succession Difference

How is top-level succession unique? To answer that question, take the case of Dennis (names in examples throughout this article have been changed). Dennis was on the fast track from the start. An Ivy League graduate, he spent three years in an industry leader's sales-training program, got his MBA at a top school, and completed a finance-training program in another industry-leading company. After 18 months, he moved to the marketing department there, then to a branch manager job for a few years. Next, he jumped to a competitor to become a country manager ("I had to get my international ticket punched"); sales records were set in his market. Five years later, he was named senior vice president for emerging markets.

Not long after that, Dennis left to become the designated CEO successor at a company in a different industry, where he was unfamiliar with the products and technology. "I wasn't looking," he said, "but I knew I could run something bigger. I was ready. I was 44 years old, and [the COO and CEO of the company I had left] were in their midfifties . . . and there were some talented people between me and them. Leaving there was the way to be a CEO faster." In business school, he had set a goal to become a CEO by age 50. "As I got closer to the top, I became more confident that I'd reach that goal. I had been in four successful companies where I'd seen CEOs up close. I'm not saying that I'm better than they were, but I knew I could do their job."

The succession plan approved by the board was for Dennis to enter as COO, with marketing, sales, manufacturing, engineering, and service reporting to him while the senior staff people (the head of HR, the CFO, and the general counsel) plus R&D stayed under Harvey, the chairman and CEO. The role of president remained unfilled. If things went well over the first 18 months, Dennis would take on that title. In another year, he would become CEO, and six months after that, Harvey would retire.

While successful over the years, Dennis's new company had seen its growth rate slow as market share eroded. "It was all about the numbers," Dennis said. "I was brought in because everyone knew I'd find a way to make them. I didn't need to know the technology as long as I could take cost out, manage the brand, and get service to be more responsive. It was right up my alley." In less than 18 months, he rationalized manufacturing, reorganized to speed up decision making, replaced many people he believed could not perform at a higher level, and helped the balance sheet through a new just-in-time inventory program. He admitted that there was more resistance to changes than he had anticipated and that Harvey had recommended moving forward more gradually and involving some of the older managers to a greater degree. Dennis complained to me: "I filled [Harvey] in on everything, and he never said no. . . . He could have vetoed any of these things, but he never did. . . . He knew that they would pay off."

But before Dennis was there two years, Harvey asked for his resignation, saying that things just hadn't worked out as everyone had hoped. He said that he and the board had decided to promote the CFO to president. Harvey did not give Dennis any feedback, explaining that there "really would be no purpose served" in doing so. He added that Dennis had brought much value for the shareholders and should feel good about what he had accomplished—that he was still young and would be a CEO somewhere.

Although the company provided a generous severance package, Dennis was angry, contending that he had been misled and used. I asked him why he believed he had failed to get the job he had so carefully prepared for. "You know, Dan," he replied, "I did all the right things . . . the things the business needed. To me, it was all because of politics. The engineering guy and the head of manufacturing and [the head] of R&D were all against the changes that I was making. . . . They wanted to keep things the way they were so they could hold on to their power . . . and they turned people against me. And Harvey doesn't like conflict. He could have told these guys to get with the plan, but he avoided that because it was going to be a tough conversation."

Dennis is a talented executive, but his reaction is a sign of why he failed. He is unlikely to reach his goal until he stops blaming others and considers what he did or did not do to cause his predicament. To start with, his conviction that making the numbers is what it takes to secure the top job is off the mark. While this is important, it's not enough to differentiate one talented CEO candidate from another. Also, Dennis's time as COO was not meant to showcase the abilities that got him to the number two spot. Rather, it was a test of his ability to manage his most important relationships and alliances. In a sense, therefore, Dennis was right—politics undid him. But political skills are essential for a CEO. Dennis neglected to see that he needed other people's help to succeed at this level and that his test was to prove he was capable of embracing a new culture, finding value in it, and appreciating perspectives other than his own. Dennis was also wrong to expect Harvey to clear away the opposition—or even to point to its existence. Understanding who must be won over to your point of view is a key part of managing the succession process.

Pitfalls of CEO Succession

When CEO hopefuls concentrate on doing more of what they have done to succeed, they typically spend too little time cultivating important relationships, especially with their bosses. Consider Vince, a manager who turned around the largest division of a struggling consumer company in less than a year. The company had developed a corporate culture where length of service counted more than performance. Vince made progress toward a performance mentality by replacing some of the people who most resisted change and introducing a performance measurement system that made it clear to those in his organization what was expected of them. At the same time, his informal style and accessibility conveyed to people that he valued them and their contributions. Employees quickly came to trust Vince and lined up behind him and what he wanted to do.

The trouble was that Vince never developed a relationship with his boss. Their regular one-on-one meetings soon became mechanical, and over time, Vince even gave up preparing for them. "He doesn't talk about strategic things. He just does check-ins on what I'm already doing," Vince complained. "It's like he thinks I'm not taking care of these things." After 18 months, discouraged that the CEO was not treating him as a successor, Vince was looking for another job. He had not stopped to analyze what the CEO paid attention to or expected from senior people. In particular, he didn't grasp that it was more important to develop a relationship with his boss than it was for his boss to create one with him. Vince didn't understand that his test was to show that he was perceptive and flexible enough to adapt to his boss's style, which differed from what he was accustomed to.

Even if would-be CEOs succeed in relating well to their bosses, some don't display enough ability to "elevate"—in other words, to gain the perspective expected of CEOs. Consider Leigh, a talented executive who had risen internally through a succession of operating management jobs in a technology-dependent manufacturing company. Because she was not an engineer, Leigh had to work harder and be more prepared than most of her technically trained peers. Although she saw it as unfair, she admitted that it had "made me a more complete, well-rounded manager. . . . I had to learn a lot more just to get my job done because I wasn't sure I could get support [I needed]." Her hard work and uncomplaining style were noticed by the CEO years before Leigh was promoted to the number two spot. "I knew what she was going through," the CEO said, "but she never showed how difficult it was for her. I think it made her tougher, more mature. . . . It broadened her; she was learning two or three jobs at a time, not just one."

But soon after Leigh became COO, her boss began to wonder whether she could handle the top job. "I didn't worry that she couldn't handle the men she beat out [now peers or subordinates] or that they'd resist doing what she told them. . . . They understood Leigh's strengths as well as I did. It's because I was not sure if she could elevate." He went on to describe complaints from Leigh's managers about not having enough freedom to run their operations. "[Her] being too controlling wasn't my experience with her, so I checked it out myself. I found out that she was jumping in to solve the problems rather than making sure her people solved them. Doing things herself was the way she had gotten ahead, but she didn't understand that at this level it was going to drag her into too much detail. If a task force was not moving fast enough, she would meet with it to get things moving instead of staying above it, laying out what had to happen, and holding the leader of the committee accountable. It was the same with her [direct reports]. If one of them came to her with a problem, she'd give him the answer instead of guiding him to find it himself." Although Leigh was "running a real tight ship, and all the right things were happening, the way she operated kept her from looking out three or four years, seeing where our [technological] edge was threatened, asking what [our major competitor] was doing that we hadn't thought about yet, and really testing her people to see if they could step up to the next level."

If they had been filled in regarding their bosses' concerns, both Vince and Leigh could have turned their situations around. But when it was suggested that Leigh's boss give her feedback, he said unenthusiastically, "I may mention it to her." Vince's boss said, "No, I want to see if Vince gets it on his own." These reactions underline a subtle reality of life at this level: Would-be CEOs can't expect much help in moving to the top spot. Boards and chief executives will give only the slightest indications of the behavior they expect. It is not that they want the number two to come in knowing all the answers. Rather, they want to see whether a candidate is sensitive to subtle cues and can adjust her behavior accordingly. CEOs and chairmen are more likely to test than to counsel.

Cue awareness is more than window dressing when it comes to trying to win the number one spot. That's because relationships at the top are so heavily scrutinized and the aspiring CEO is always in the spotlight. At this level, a senior manager gets an edge by being concerned with what is best for the whole company as well as with what's good for the units that report to her. Take Helen, a leader in a large, global corporation at the head of its industry. Some saw her as the logical successor to the CEO. She had strong interpersonal skills complemented by charm and humility—rare qualities in her company. Her climb up the ladder was swift; in her mid-forties, she was reporting to the CEO and running the most profitable part of the corporation. That's when Helen's career plateaued.

Her CEO explained that she was "important to this company in so many ways, but one big reason that she could probably never be a CEO was the downside of loyalty." Although she often talked about the need for teamwork among her peers, she didn't always act as a team player. She made loyalty to her and her agenda the price of admission to her inner circle. She resisted allowing her better people to move to other parts of the corporation, especially if it meant they would be working for another CEO contender. The CEO had a few concerns about her. First, her behavior revealed that she cared more about the success of her own unit than about the success of the organization overall. Second, she kept her better people from jobs in other areas of the company, denying them chances to broaden themselves and robbing other departments of new talent. Third, while she enjoyed intense loyalty within her organization, she had not gained the political support from her peers she would need as CEO, nor had she seeded other parts of the organization with people who knew her well and could help her when she needed it.

Good CEOs and boards are experts at assessing an aspiring CEO's ability to master the nuances of the top job. For Dennis, the test was to find value in the culture of the company whose performance he was improving; for Vince, to gauge what was important to his boss; for Leigh, to point people toward solutions rather than solving all the problems herself; and for Helen, to help others succeed and to concentrate on improving the organization as a whole, not just her unit. These potential successors did not understand the tests they faced, so they missed subtle cues and were set back in their quest for the top position.

Winning Criteria

Each of the designated successors in the examples above failed to establish sufficient credibility for their bosses to stand aside. The signs that they were failing were not easy for them to recognize because they were well matched with the strategic and technical needs of their jobs; indeed, these people were talented, accomplished managers who contributed much to their organizations. What extra ingredients should they have brought? What criteria should CEOs and boards use in judging CEO candidates? (For a more complete list, see the exhibit "The Winner's Difference.")

Watching and analyzing successes and failures at the number two level suggests that executives vary in the degree to which they have the qualifications to win the top job. At one end of the spectrum are managers who have the capabilities they need to be considered as CEOs. Managers on the other end, however, are the elite few who have honed these capabilities with the subtlety and sophistication required for operating effectively at the CEO level.

The capabilities fall into a few broad categories. The first set has to do with senior management best practices—for example, the ability to prioritize the things that will make the difference operationally. At this level, managers must use time wisely, delegate the right tasks, and develop people; these are basic abilities expected of everyone. But the people who make it to the top tend to proceed in subtly different ways than do the senior man-

The Winner's Difference

The following table lists the capabilities of people who have a good chance of becoming CEO—and what elite candidates do in addition in order to get the edge.

	The Good Candidate:	The Elite Candidate:
Management Savvy	· knows what is required operationally for short-term results · motivates others to do it · uses time well · prioritizes among issues that are all important · frequently delegates tasks · has a history of developing subordinates and exporting talent · organizes and mobilizes talent toward most significant problems · pushes people to achieve more than they think they can	· avoids jumping in personally to solve problems others can handle · makes the right judgments about what to expend energy on · maintains control of the key decisions and a full pipeline of talented people · makes people feel appreciated and stay loyal
Political Intelligence	· accurately reads political currents · understands patterns of relationships quickly in an unfamiliar environment · builds relationships with peers and subordinates · makes sure the CEO and the board know what he or she is capable of doing	· isn't labeled "political" · recognizes how relationships are likely to affect early success · gets peers and subordinates to go out of their way to help · doesn't seem self-serving
Personal Style	· is a star performer · is intense and driven to excel · is hardworking, usually putting in more time and effort than peers do · enthusiastically backs initiatives that will help the business succeed · is a leader among peers · understands new ways of doing things and makes important connections	· makes success look effortless · allows others' performance to be recognized, too · manages energy to stay on the "rested edge" and to avoid the "ragged edge" · knows when to hold back and when to let go · enables peers to improve their performance · stays grounded and makes sure basic needs are met while mastering new concepts

agers who remain stuck at number two. For instance, winners know what is required for short-term results, and they can direct others to do it. But unlike Leigh, they avoid getting too involved in solving problems that others should handle.

The second set of capabilities has to do with managing the political environment. At the less-sophisticated end of the spectrum are those who accurately read most political currents, while those with better-honed abilities will do so in a way that avoids their being labeled "political." Most senior executives build good working relationships with peers (which Helen did), but the ones who become CEOs garner active peer support. Often, their peers and subordinates will go out of their way to offer feedback or to point out potential problems (which Helen's colleagues didn't do). Most people close to the top also know how to show the CEO and the board what they are capable of doing. But the ones who don't make it to the number one job tend to believe that they haven't received the recognition they deserve. (This is true of both Vince and Dennis.) As a result, they come across as too concerned with getting credit. Executives at the other end of the continuum receive credit by finding ways for their virtues to be touted by others, so they don't need to shine the spotlight of attention too brightly on themselves.

The third category has to do with personal style. The number two works hard, sacrificing personal time and expending significant effort to achieve impressive results. But the winner never makes a big deal of the success he is responsible for (unlike Dennis and Vince). Of course, being intensely competitive and driven to be the best is a given among high-level managers, but those who are furthest along the spectrum manage to give credit to others involved in successes without diminishing their own recognition. Being a leader among peers is what all senior executives have done to get where they are; elite executives have learned how to do it so that their peers become better performers.

Rules of Engagement

Success at winning the CEO title always depends on the situation, the organizational culture, the types of people and relationships involved, and the personality and style of the candidate. While there are no hard-and-fast rules, a few basic guidelines can help the aspiring CEO shape his own destiny.

UNDERSTAND THE BOSS'S POINT OF VIEW

Whether the CEO has earned your respect is not the issue here. All that matters is that you respect his position and get to know what is important to him. Start by understanding what contributed most to his success: Who helped him along the way, and are those advisers still valuable to him? How did he handle failures?

Then try to understand the type of person he is. What is his leadership style and approach to decision making? What types of questions does he ask? Does he ask questions to verify what he has concluded or to gain input he has not considered? How does he respond to the answers? Does he tend to make decisions by talking with people one-on-one or in a group? Also, search for clues that indicate the best way to relate to him. Which people influence him the most? How does he manage their advice? How does he want to be kept informed? What behavior does he expect from senior people? How does the boss's style differ from yours and from the styles of others you have worked for?

It's essential to appreciate how difficult it is for him to hand over the reins. Years ago, I was the designated successor for a CEO who I believe was passing the chairman and CEO titles to me only reluctantly. I was determined to work harder and be more productive so he would have no excuse to back away. The founder of the Boston Consulting Group, Bruce Henderson (who had retired and thus gone through his own transfer of power to a successor), was one of my advisers. When I asked him for feedback on what I should be doing differently, I expected a pearl of strategic wisdom about accelerating top-line growth to increase our market share. But he simply said, "Be more understanding about what [the chairman] is going through." Instead of thinking that Bruce had lost a bit of his edge and being disappointed that he did not say something about what I was going through, I should have taken the time to understand what he meant. If I had, my transition would have gone more smoothly.

KNOW YOUR LIMITATIONS

There are many incentives for board members, CEOs, HR people, or executive search consultants to encourage a potential CEO to believe that he is more prepared than he really is. While these people are often well-intentioned, if he believes them, he might pay too little attention to cultivating the particular abilities most important for his success.

Take the case of Wayne, who moved from a *Fortune* 50 global corporation to a smaller company because of the opportunity to become CEO years earlier than if he had stayed put. The incumbent chairman and CEO was ill, and the lead director of the board had taken over most of his duties. Wayne was recruited aggressively by the board members, partly because he had much of what they believed their company needed, but also because the corporation where he had become a rising star was among the world's best performers and was known for producing very good managers. The board reasoned that Wayne would impress investors and employees alike.

In his first year after joining, Wayne worked hard to master new technologies, markets, and customers. He learned how to impress analysts and institutional investors. His operational skills turned out to be just what the company needed, bringing remarkable bottom-line results and cost savings. His upbeat style was refreshing, and his encouragement to try new approaches motivated employees to innovate at a rate the company had not seen before. After 11 months, the lead director said, "The board believes things are going really well and wants to accelerate your move up to CEO . . . . You're our guy."

Wayne was surprised, pleased, and anxious all at the same time. He appreciated the vote of confidence, but, although he took care not to appear as though he believed the top job exceeded his capabilities, he was unsure that he was ready for such a step. He was still learning the business, and there were challenges (such as acquisitions and technical alliances) with which he had little direct experience and where the managers in charge had not impressed him.

Over the next month, several of the directors spent more time meeting with Wayne than they had in his entire tenure at the company. At first he thought they

were testing him, but he soon realized that they were trying to persuade him to take the CEO spot. They were selling.

Wayne lasted 15 months as CEO. He was not ready
and should have stayed in the number two spot for
another couple of years. It is difficult to blame him for
taking the opportunity to be CEO—his failure was really
more the fault of the board. Eventually, he would have
had the self-confidence and experience to be very effective as head of that company. The board members were
more concerned about image and getting someone in the
CEO spot quickly. In other words, they cared more about
what was good for the board than about what was good
for Wayne or even the company.

MANAGE THE SHADOW ORGANIZATION

In order to get a CEO position, it's important to grasp the
alliances and political realities that aren't apparent right
away but come with top-level jobs. Whether entering a
new organization or being promoted to headquarters,
the wise manager will find ways to understand how this
often-hidden network of relationships and norms can
influence her success.

One way to gain such understanding is to trace the
histories of successes and failures. Who were the people
most responsible, and what happened to them? How did
they help form influential groups? What patterns of loyalty emerged? Were there attempts to isolate lessons and
ensure they were understood? Is such learning reflected
in who has been hired, in performance management, and
in training and development programs? In getting to the
core of reality, it is useful to look to Japanese manufac-
turers of the 1970s. They adopted the habit of asking

"why" five times when they discovered an important production or distribution problem, because they believed that root causes lay at least four levels below the surface.

Another way to grasp the political climate is to understand what is actually valued. Most CEOs have endorsed a list of values that are prominently displayed on office walls. In most cases, though, these bear little resemblance to actual behavior or to how the most important decisions are made. To determine whether values are meaningful, find out how they came into existence. They mean something when they have been created over a long period, evolving from ethical wins and mistakes. They stand the test of time. The most cherished are passed from one generation to the next. Values are sure to be superficial, however, when they have been created by outsiders for a fee. Here is a particularly ironic example: One company unveiled a new set of values written by a consulting firm that in the same week admitted its role in another client's financial scandal.

• • •

Most people who get close to the top are talented, hardworking, and smart enough to go all the way—but fail because they don't know how to approach this entirely new challenge. A good number of these failures are avoidable. That we have allowed this to happen in organizations that are otherwise excellent performers is a disgrace; it exacts a huge cost in terms of time, money, and wasted potential. The price is paid by many people: employees depending on a smooth handoff at the top, investors expecting continuous leadership, and families uprooted when jobs do not work out as hoped. Among those at fault are boards of directors that do not oversee the succession process or hold CEOs accountable for a smooth transition, human resource organizations that should have the capacity to help but are not up to the task, and CEOs who do a poor job of coaching potential successors.

In spite of these obstacles, the aspiring CEO can dramatically increase his chances of success by sharpening his perception of the organization's culture and politics, by mastering the art of building winning relationships, and by improving his self-awareness. Most of all, he must learn to conduct himself with the maturity and wisdom that demonstrate to those making the decision that he is, indeed, ready.

Originally published in January 2005
Reprint R0501D

Overloaded Circuits

Why Smart People Underperform

EDWARD M. HALLOWELL

Executive Summary

FRENZIED EXECUTIVES WHO FIDGET through meetings, lose track of their appointments, and jab at the "door close" button on the elevator aren't crazy—just crazed. They suffer from a newly recognized neurological phenomenon that the author, a psychiatrist, calls attention deficit trait, or ADT. It isn't an illness; it's purely a response to the hyperkinetic environment in which we live. But it has become epidemic in today's organizations.

When a manager is desperately trying to deal with more input than he possibly can, the brain and body get locked into a reverberating circuit while the brain's frontal lobes lose their sophistication, as if vinegar were added to wine. The result is black-and-white thinking; perspective and shades of gray disappear. People with ADT have difficulty staying organized, setting priorities, and managing time, and they feel a constant low level of panic and guilt.

ADT can be controlled by engineering one's environment and one's emotional and physical health. Make time every few hours for a "human moment," a face-to-face exchange with a person you like. Get enough sleep, switch to a good diet, and get adequate exercise. Break down large tasks into smaller ones, and keep a section of your work space clear. Try keeping a portion of your day free of appointments and e-mail.

The author recommends that companies invest in amenities that contribute to a positive atmosphere. Leaders can also help prevent ADT by matching employees' skills to tasks. When managers assign goals that stretch people too far or ask workers to focus on what they're not good at, stress rises. ADT is a very real threat to all of us. If we don't manage it, it will manage us.

D AVID DRUMS HIS FINGERS on his desk as he scans the e-mail on his computer screen. At the same time, he's talking on the phone to an executive halfway around the world. His knee bounces up and down like a jackhammer. He intermittently bites his lip and reaches for his constant companion, the coffee cup. He's so deeply involved in multitasking that he has forgotten the appointment his Outlook calendar reminded him of 15 minutes ago.

Jane, a senior vice president, and Mike, her CEO, have adjoining offices so they can communicate quickly, yet communication never seems to happen. "Whenever I go into Mike's office, his phone lights up, my cell phone goes off, someone knocks on the door, he suddenly turns to his screen and writes an e-mail, or he tells me about a new issue he wants me to address," Jane complains. "We're working flat out just to stay afloat, and we're not getting anything important accomplished. It's driving me crazy."

David, Jane, and Mike aren't crazy, but they're certainly crazed. Their experience is becoming the norm for overworked managers who suffer—like many of your colleagues, and possibly like you—from a very real but unrecognized neurological phenomenon that I call attention deficit trait, or ADT. Caused by brain overload, ADT is now epidemic in organizations. The core symptoms are distractibility, inner frenzy, and impatience. People with ADT have difficulty staying organized, setting priorities, and managing time. These symptoms can undermine the work of an otherwise gifted executive. If David, Jane, Mike, and the millions like them understood themselves in neurological terms, they could actively manage their lives instead of reacting to problems as they happen.

As a psychiatrist who has diagnosed and treated thousands of people over the past 25 years for a medical condition called attention deficit disorder, or ADD (now known clinically as attention-deficit/hyperactivity disorder), I have observed firsthand how a rapidly growing segment of the adult population is developing this new, related condition. The number of people with ADT coming into my clinical practice has mushroomed by a factor of ten in the past decade. Unfortunately, most of the remedies for chronic overload proposed by time-management consultants and executive coaches do not address the underlying causes of ADT.

Unlike ADD, a neurological disorder that has a genetic component and can be aggravated by environmental and physical factors, ADT springs entirely from the environment. Like the traffic jam, ADT is an artifact of modern life. It is brought on by the demands on our time and attention that have exploded over the past two decades. As our minds fill with noise—feckless synaptic events signifying nothing—the brain gradually loses its capacity to attend fully and thoroughly to anything.

The symptoms of ADT come upon a person gradually. The sufferer doesn't experience a single crisis but rather a series of minor emergencies while he or she tries harder and harder to keep up. Shouldering a responsibility to "suck it up" and not complain as the workload increases, executives with ADT do whatever they can to handle a load they simply cannot manage as well as they'd like. The ADT sufferer therefore feels a constant low level of panic and guilt. Facing a tidal wave of tasks, the executive becomes increasingly hurried, curt, peremptory, and unfocused, while pretending that everything is fine.

To control ADT, we first have to recognize it. And control it we must, if we as individuals and organizational leaders are to be effective. In the following pages, I'll offer an analysis of the origins of ADT and provide some suggestions that may help you manage it.

Attention Deficit Cousins

To understand the nature and treatment of ADT, it's useful to know something of its cousin, ADD.

Usually seen as a learning disability in children, ADD also afflicts about 5% of the adult population. Researchers using MRI scans have found that people with ADD suffer a slightly diminished volume in four specific brain regions that have various functions such as modulating emotion (especially anger and frustration) and assisting in learning. One of the regions, made up of the frontal and prefrontal lobes, generates thoughts, makes decisions, sets priorities, and organizes activities. While the medications used to treat ADD don't change the anatomy of the brain, they alter brain chemistry, which in turn improves function in each of the four regions and so dramatically bolsters the performance of ADD sufferers.

ADD confers both disadvantages and advantages. The negative characteristics include a tendency to procrastinate and miss deadlines. People with ADD struggle with disorganization and tardiness; they can be forgetful and drift away mentally in the middle of a conversation or while reading. Their performance can be inconsistent: brilliant one moment and unsatisfactory the next. ADD sufferers also tend to demonstrate impatience and lose focus unless, oddly enough, they are under stress or handling multiple inputs. (This is because stress leads to the production of adrenaline, which is chemically similar to the medications we use to treat ADD.) Finally, people with ADD sometimes also self-medicate with excessive alcohol or other substances.

On the positive side, those with ADD usually possess rare talents and gifts. Those gifts often go unnoticed or undeveloped, however, because of the problems caused by the condition's negative symptoms. ADD sufferers can be remarkably creative and original. They are unusually persistent under certain circumstances and often possess an entrepreneurial flair. They display ingenuity and encourage that trait in others. They tend to improvise well under pressure. Because they have the ability to field multiple inputs simultaneously, they can be strong leaders during times of change. They also tend to rebound quickly after setbacks and bring fresh energy to the company every day.

Executives with ADD typically achieve inconsistent results. Sometimes they fail miserably because they're disorganized and make mistakes. At other times, they perform brilliantly, offering original ideas and strategies that lead to performance at the highest level.

David Neeleman, the CEO of JetBlue Airways, has ADD. School was torture; unable to focus, he hated to study and procrastinated endlessly. "I felt like I should be out doing things, moving things along, but here I was, stuck studying statistics, which I knew had no application to my life," Neeleman told me. "I knew I had to have an education, but at the first opportunity to start a business, I just blew out of college." He climbed quickly in the corporate world, making use of his strengths—original thinking, high energy, an ability to draw out the best in people—and getting help with organization and time management.

Like most people with ADD, Neeleman could sometimes offend with his blunt words, but his ideas were good enough to change the airline industry. For example, he invented the electronic ticket. "When I proposed that idea, people laughed at me, saying no one would go to the airport without a paper ticket," he says. "Now everyone does, and it has saved the industry millions of dollars." It seems fitting that someone with ADD would invent a way around having to remember to bring a paper ticket. Neeleman believes ADD is one of the keys to his success. Far from regretting having it, he celebrates it. But he understands that he must manage his ADD carefully.

Attention deficit trait is characterized by ADD's negative symptoms. Rather than being rooted in genetics, however, ADT is purely a response to the hyperkinetic environment in which we live. Indeed, modern culture all but requires many of us to develop ADT. Never in history has the human brain been asked to track so many data points. Everywhere, people rely on their cell phones, e-mail, and digital assistants in the race to gather and transmit data, plans, and ideas faster and faster. One could argue that the chief value of the modern era is speed, which the novelist Milan Kundera described as "the form of ecstasy that technology has bestowed upon modern man." Addicted to speed, we demand it even when we can't possibly go faster. James Gleick wryly noted in *Faster: The Acceleration of Just About Everything* that the "close door" button in elevators is often the one with the paint worn off. As the human brain struggles to keep up, it falters and then falls into the world of ADT.

This Is Your Brain

While brain scans cannot display anatomical differences between people with "normal" brains and people suffering from ADT, studies have shown that as the human brain is asked to process dizzying amounts of data, its ability to solve problems flexibly and creatively declines and the number of mistakes increases. To find out why, let's go on a brief neurological journey.

Blessed with the largest cortex in all of nature, owners of this trillion-celled organ today put singular pressure on the frontal and prefrontal lobes, which I'll refer to in this article as simply the frontal lobes. This region governs what is called, aptly enough, executive functioning (EF). EF guides decision making and planning; the organization and prioritization of information and ideas;

time management; and various other sophisticated, uniquely human, managerial tasks. As long as our frontal lobes remain in charge, everything is fine.

Beneath the frontal lobes lie the parts of the brain devoted to survival. These deep centers govern basic functions like sleep, hunger, sexual desire, breathing, and heart rate, as well as crudely positive and negative emotions. When you are doing well and operating at peak level, the deep centers send up messages of excitement, satisfaction, and joy. They pump up your motivation, help you maintain attention, and don't interfere with working memory, the number of data points you can keep track of at once. But when you are confronted with the sixth decision after the fifth interruption in the midst of a search for the ninth missing piece of information on the day that the third deal has collapsed and the 12th impossible request has blipped unbidden across your computer screen, your brain begins to panic, reacting just as if that sixth decision were a bloodthirsty, man-eating tiger.

As a specialist in learning disabilities, I have found that the most dangerous disability is not any formally diagnosable condition like dyslexia or ADD. It is fear. Fear shifts us into survival mode and thus prevents fluid learning and nuanced understanding. Certainly, if a real tiger is about to attack you, survival is the mode you want to be in. But if you're trying to deal intelligently with a subtle task, survival mode is highly unpleasant and counterproductive.

When the frontal lobes approach capacity and we begin to fear that we can't keep up, the relationship between the higher and lower regions of the brain takes an ominous turn. Thousands of years of evolution have taught the higher brain not to ignore the lower brain's distress signals. In survival mode, the deep areas of the brain assume control and begin to direct the higher regions. As a result, the whole brain gets caught in a neurological catch-22. The deep regions interpret the messages of overload they receive from the frontal lobes in the same way they interpret everything: primitively. They furiously fire signals of fear, anxiety, impatience, irritability, anger, or panic. These alarm signals shanghai the attention of the frontal lobes, forcing them to forfeit much of their power. Because survival signals are irresistible, the frontal lobes get stuck sending messages back to the deep centers saying, "Message received. Trying to work on it but without success." These messages further perturb the deep centers, which send even more powerful messages of distress back up to the frontal lobes.

Meanwhile, in response to what's going on in the brain, the rest of the body—particularly the endocrine, respiratory, cardiovascular, musculoskeletal, and peripheral nervous systems—has shifted into crisis mode and changed its baseline physiology from peace and quiet to red alert. The brain and body are locked in a reverberating circuit while the frontal lobes lose their sophistication, as if vinegar were added to wine. In this state, EF reverts to simpleminded black-and-white thinking; perspective and shades of gray disappear. Intelligence dims. In a futile attempt to do more than is possible, the brain paradoxically reduces its ability to think clearly.

This neurological event occurs when a manager is desperately trying to deal with more input than he possibly can. In survival mode, the manager makes impulsive judgments, angrily rushing to bring closure to whatever matter is at hand. He feels compelled to get the problem under control immediately, to extinguish the perceived danger lest it destroy him. He is robbed of his flexibility, his sense of humor, his ability to deal with the unknown. He forgets the big picture and the goals and values he stands for. He loses his creativity and his ability to change plans. He desperately wants to kill the metaphorical tiger. At these moments he is prone to melting down, to throwing a tantrum, to blaming others, and to sabotaging himself. Or he may go in the opposite direction, falling into denial and total avoidance of the problems attacking him, only to be devoured. This is ADT at its worst.

Though ADT does not always reach such extreme proportions, it does wreak havoc among harried workers. Because no two brains are alike, some people deal with the condition better than others. Regardless of how well executives appear to function, however, no one has total control over his or her executive functioning.

Managing ADT

Unfortunately, top management has so far viewed the symptoms of ADT through the distorting lens of morality or character. Employees who seem unable to keep up the pace are seen as deficient or weak. Consider the case of an executive who came to see me when he was completely overloaded. I suggested he talk the situation over with his superior and ask for help. When my client did so, he was told that if he couldn't handle the work, he ought to think about resigning. Even though his performance assessments were stellar and he'd earned praise for being one of the most creative people in the organization, he was allowed to leave. Because the firm sought to preserve the myth that no straw would ever break its people's backs, it could not tolerate the manager's stating that his back was breaking. After he went out on his own, he flourished.

How can we control the rampaging effects of ADT, both in ourselves and in our organizations? While ADD often requires medication, the treatment of ADT certainly does not. ADT can be controlled only by creatively engineering one's environment and one's emotional and physical health. I have found that the following preventive measures go a long way toward helping executives control their symptoms of ADT.

PROMOTE POSITIVE EMOTIONS

The most important step in controlling ADT is not to buy a superturbocharged BlackBerry and fill it up with to-dos but rather to create an environment in which the brain can function at its best. This means building a positive, fear-free emotional atmosphere, because emotion is the on/off switch for executive functioning.

There are neurological reasons why ADT occurs less in environments where people are in physical contact and where they trust and respect one another. When you comfortably connect with a colleague, even if you are dealing with an overwhelming problem, the deep centers of the brain send messages through the pleasure center to the area that assigns resources to the frontal lobes. Even when you're under extreme stress, this sense of human connection causes executive functioning to hum.

By contrast, people who work in physical isolation are more likely to suffer from ADT, for the more isolated we are, the more stressed we become. I witnessed a dramatic example of the danger of a disconnected environment and the healing power of a connected one when I consulted for one of the world's foremost university chemistry departments. In the department's formerly hard-driven culture, ADT was rampant, exacerbated by an ethic that forbade anyone to ask for help or even state that anything was wrong. People did not trust one another; they worked on projects alone, which led to more mistrust. Most people were in emotional pain, but implicit in the department's culture was the notion that great pain led to great gain.

In the late 1990s, one of the department's most gifted graduate students killed himself. His suicide note explicitly blamed the university for pushing him past his limit. The department's culture was literally lethal.

Instead of trying to sweep the tragedy under the rug, the chair of the department and his successor acted boldly and creatively. They immediately changed the structure of the supervisory system so that each graduate student and postdoc was assigned three supervisors, rather than a single one with a death grip on the trainee's career. The department set up informal biweekly buffets that allowed people to connect. (Even the most reclusive chemist came out of hiding for food, one of life's great connectors.) The department heads went as far as changing the architecture of the department's main building, taking down walls and adding common areas and an espresso bar complete with a grand piano. They provided lectures and written information to all students about the danger signs of mental wear and tear and offered confidential procedures for students who needed help. These steps, along with regular meetings that included senior faculty and university administrators, led to a more humane, productive culture in which the students and faculty felt fully engaged. The department's performance remained first-rate, and creative research blossomed.

The bottom line is this: Fostering connections and reducing fear promote brainpower. When you make time at least every four to six hours for a "human moment," a face-to-face exchange with a person you like, you are giving your brain what it needs.

TAKE PHYSICAL CARE OF YOUR BRAIN

Sleep, a good diet, and exercise are critical for staving off ADT. Though this sounds like a no-brainer, too many of us abuse our brains by neglecting obvious principles of care.

You may try to cope with ADT by sleeping less, in the vain hope that you can get more done. This is the opposite of what you need to do, for ADT sets in when you don't get enough sleep. There is ample documentation to suggest that sleep deprivation engenders a host of problems, from impaired decision making and reduced creativity to reckless behavior and paranoia. We vary in how much sleep we require; a good rule of thumb is that you're getting enough sleep if you can wake up without an alarm clock.

Diet also plays a crucial role in brain health. Many hardworking people habitually inhale carbohydrates, which cause blood glucose levels to yo-yo. This leads to a vicious cycle: Rapid fluctuations in insulin levels further increase the craving for carbohydrates. The brain, which relies on glucose for energy, is left either glutted or gasping, neither of which makes for optimal cognitive functioning.

The brain does much better if the blood glucose level can be held relatively stable. To do this, avoid simple carbohydrates containing sugar and white flour (pastries, white bread, and pasta, for example). Rely on the complex carbohydrates found in fruits, whole grains, and vegetables. Protein is important: Instead of starting your day with coffee and a Danish, try tea and an egg or a piece of smoked salmon on wheat toast. Take a multivitamin every day as well as supplementary omega-3 fatty acids, an excellent source of which is fish oil. The omega-3s and the E and B complex contained in multivitamins promote healthy brain function and may even stave off Alzheimer's disease and inflammatory ills (which can be the starting point for major killers like heart disease, stroke, diabetes, and cancer). Moderate your intake of alcohol, too, because too much kills brain cells and accelerates the development of memory loss and even dementia. As you change your diet to promote optimal brain function and good general health, your body will also shed excess pounds.

If you think you can't afford the time to exercise, think again. Sitting at a desk for hours on end decreases mental acuity, not only because of reduced blood flow to the brain but for other biochemical reasons as well. Physical exercise induces the body to produce an array of chemicals that the brain loves, including endorphins, serotonin, dopamine, epinephrine, and norepinephrine, as well as two recently discovered compounds, brain-derived neurotrophic factor (BDNF) and nerve growth factor (NGF). Both BDNF and NGF promote cell health and development in the brain, stave off the ravages of aging and stress, and keep the brain in tip-top condition. Nothing stimulates the production of BDNF and NGF as robustly as physical exercise, which explains why those who exercise regularly talk about the letdown and sluggishness they experience if they miss their exercise for a few days. You will more than compensate for the time you invest on the treadmill with improved productivity and efficiency. To fend off the symptoms of ADT while you're at work, get up from your desk and go up and down a flight of stairs a few times or walk briskly down a hallway. These quick, simple efforts will push your brain's reset button.

ORGANIZE FOR ADT

It's important to develop tactics for getting organized, but not in the sense of empty New Year's resolutions. Rather, your goal is to order your work in a way that suits you, so that disorganization does not keep you from reaching your goals.

First, devise strategies to help your frontal lobes stay in control. These might include breaking down large tasks into smaller ones and keeping a section of your work space or desk clear at all times. (You do not need to have a neat office, just a neat section of your office.) Similarly, you might try keeping a portion of your day free of appointments, e-mail, and other distractions so that you have time to think and plan. Because e-mail is a wonderful way to procrastinate and set yourself up for ADT at the same time, you might consider holding specific "e-mail hours," since it isn't necessary to reply to every e-mail right away.

When you start your day, don't allow yourself to get sucked into vortices of e-mail or voice mail or into attending to minor tasks that eat up your time but don't pack a punch. Attend to a critical task instead. Before you leave for the day, make a list of no more than five priority items that will require your attention tomorrow. Short lists force you to prioritize and complete your tasks. Additionally, keep torrents of documents at bay. One of my patients, an executive with ADD, uses the

OHIO rule: Only handle it once. If he touches a document, he acts on it, files it, or throws it away. "I don't put it in a pile," he says. "Piles are like weeds. If you let them grow, they take over everything."

Pay attention to the times of day when you feel that you perform at your best; do your most important work then and save the rote work for other times. Set up your office in a way that helps mental functioning. If you focus better with music, have music (if need be, use earphones). If you think best on your feet, work standing up or walk around frequently. If doodling or drumming your fingers helps, figure out a way to do so without bothering anyone, or get a fidget toy to bring to meetings. These small strategies sound mundane, but they address the ADT devil that resides in distracting details.

PROTECT YOUR FRONTAL LOBES

To stay out of survival mode and keep your lower brain from usurping control, slow down. Take the time you need to comprehend what is going on, to listen, to ask questions, and to digest what's been said so that you don't get confused and send your brain into panic. Empower an assistant to ride herd on you; insist that he or she tell you to stop e-mailing, get off the telephone, or leave the office.

If you do begin to feel overwhelmed, try the following mind-clearing tricks. Do an easy rote task, such as resetting the calendar on your watch or writing a memo on a neutral topic. If you feel anxious about beginning a project, pull out a sheet of paper or fire up your word processor and write a paragraph about something unrelated to the project (a description of your house, your car, your shoes—anything you know well). You can also tackle the easiest part of the task; for example, write just the title of a memo about it. Open a dictionary and read a few definitions, or spend five minutes doing a crossword puzzle. Each of these little tasks quiets your lower brain by tricking it into shutting off alarmist messages and puts your frontal lobes back in full control.

Finally, be ready for the next attack of ADT by posting the sidebar "Control Your ADT" near your desk where you can see it. Knowing that you are prepared diminishes the likelihood of an attack, because you're not susceptible to panic.

What Leaders Can Do

All too often, companies induce and exacerbate ADT in their employees by demanding fast thinking rather than deep thinking. Firms also ask employees to work on multiple overlapping projects and initiatives, resulting in second-rate thinking. Worse, companies that ask their employees to do too much at once tend to reward those who say yes to overload while punishing those who choose to focus and say no.

Moreover, organizations make the mistake of forcing their employees to do more and more with less and less by eliminating support staff. Such companies end up losing money in the long run, for the more time a manager has to spend being his own administrative assistant and the less he is able to delegate, the less effective he will be in doing the important work of moving the organization forward. Additionally, firms that ignore the symptoms of ADT in their employees suffer its ill effects: Employees underachieve, create clutter, cut corners, make careless mistakes, and squander their brainpower. As demands continue to increase, a toxic, high-pressure environment leads to high rates of employee illness and turnover.

To counteract ADT and harness employee brain-power, firms should invest in amenities that contribute to a positive atmosphere. One company that has done an excellent job in this regard is SAS Institute, a major software company in North Carolina. The company famously offers its employees a long list of perks: a 36,000-square-foot, on-site gym; a seven-hour workday that ends at 5 PM; the largest on-site day care facility in North Carolina; a cafeteria that provides baby seats and high chairs so parents can eat lunch with their children; unlimited sick days; and much more. The atmosphere at SAS is warm, connected, and relaxed. The effect on the bottom line is profoundly positive; turnover is never higher than 5%. The company saves the millions other software companies spend on recruiting, training, and severance (estimated to be at least 1.5 times salary in the software industry). Employees return the favors with high productivity. The forces of ADT that shred other organizations never gain momentum at SAS.

Leaders can also help prevent ADT by matching employees' skills to tasks. When managers assign goals that stretch people too far or ask workers to focus on what they're not good at rather than what they do well, stress rises. By contrast, managers who understand the dangers of ADT can find ways of keeping themselves and their organizations on track. JetBlue's David Neeleman, for example, has shamelessly and publicly identified what he is not good at and found ways to deal with his shortcomings, either by delegating or by empowering his assistant to direct him. Neeleman also models this behavior for everyone else in the organization. His openness about the challenges of his ADD gives others permission to speak about their own attention deficit difficulties and to garner the support they need. He also encourages his managers to match people with tasks that fit their cognitive and emotional styles, knowing that no one style is best. Neeleman believes that helping people work to their strengths is not just a mark of sophisticated management; it's also an excellent way to boost worker productivity and morale.

• • •

ADT is a very real threat to all of us. If we do not manage it, it manages us. But an understanding of ADT and its ravages allows us to apply practical methods to improve our work and our lives. In the end, the most critical step an enlightened leader can take to address the problem of ADT is to name it. Bringing ADT out of the closet and describing its symptoms removes the stigma and eliminates the moral condemnation companies have for so long mistakenly leveled at overburdened employees. By giving people permission to ask for help and remaining vigilant for signs of stress, organizations will go a long way toward fostering more productive, well-balanced, and intelligent work environments.

Control Your ADT

In General

- Get adequate sleep.
- Watch what you eat. Avoid simple, sugary carbohydrates, moderate your intake of alcohol, add protein, stick to complex carbohydrates (vegetables, whole grains, fruit).

- Exercise at least 30 minutes at least every other day.
- Take a daily multivitamin and an omega-3 fatty acid supplement.

At Work

- Do all you can to create a trusting, connected work environment.
- Have a friendly, face-to-face talk with a person you like every four to six hours.
- Break large tasks into smaller ones.
- Keep a section of your work space or desk clear at all times.
- Each day, reserve some "think time" that's free from appointments, e-mail, and phone calls.
- Set aside e-mail until you've completed at least one or two more important tasks.
- Before you leave work each day, create a short list of three to five items you will attend to the next day.
- Try to act on, file, or toss every document you touch.
- Don't let papers accumulate.
- Pay attention to the times of day when you feel that you are at your best; do your most important work then, and save the rote work for other times.
- Do whatever you need to do to work in a more focused way: Add background music, walk around, and so on.
- Ask a colleague or an assistant to help you stop talking on the telephone, e-mailing, or working too late.

When You Feel Overwhelmed

- Slow down.
- Do an easy rote task: Reset your watch, write a note about a neutral topic (such as a description of your

house), read a few dictionary definitions, do a short crossword puzzle.

- Move around: Go up and down a flight of stairs or walk briskly.

- Ask for help, delegate a task, or brainstorm with a colleague. In short, do not worry alone.

Originally published in January 2005
Reprint R0501E

What's Your Story?

HERMINIA IBARRA AND KENT LINEBACK

Executive Summary

WHEN YOU'RE IN THE MIDST of a major career change, telling stories about your professional self can inspire others' belief in your character and in your capacity to take a leap and land on your feet. It also can help you believe in yourself. A narrative thread will give meaning to your career history; it will assure you that, in moving on to something new, you are not discarding everything you've worked so hard to accomplish.

Unfortunately, the authors explain in this article, most of us fail to use the power of storytelling in pursuit of our professional goals, or we do it badly. Tales of transition are especially challenging. Not knowing how to reconcile the built-in discontinuities in our work lives, we often relay just the facts. We present ourselves as safe—and dull and unremarkable.

That's not a necessary compromise. A transition story has inherent dramatic appeal. The protagonist is you, of course, and what's at stake is your career. Perhaps you've come to an event or insight that represents a point of no return. It's this kind of break with the past that will force you to discover and reveal who you really are. Discontinuity and tension are part of the experience. If these elements are missing from your career story, the tale will fall flat.

With all these twists and turns, how do you demonstrate stability and earn listeners' trust? By emphasizing continuity and causality—in other words, by showing that your past is related to the present and, from that trajectory, conveying that a solid future is in sight. If you can make your story of transition cohere, you will have gone far in convincing the listener—and reassuring yourself—that the change makes sense for you and is likely to bring success.

A$_{\text{T A RECENT NETWORKING EVENT}}$, senior managers who'd been downsized out of high-paying corporate jobs took turns telling what they had done before and what they were looking for next. Person after person stood up and recounted a laundry list of credentials and jobs, in chronological order. Many felt compelled to begin with their first job, some even with their place of birth. The accounting was meticulous.

Most people spent their allotted two minutes (and lost the attention of those around them) before they even reached the punch line—the description of what they were seeking. Those who did leave time to wrap up tended merely to list the four or five (disparate) things they might be interested in pursuing next. In the feed-back sessions that followed each round of presentations, these "fact tellers" were hard to help. The people listening couldn't readily understand how their knowledge and contacts might bear upon the teller's situation. Even worse, they didn't feel compelled to try very hard.

In our research and coaching on career reorientation, we've witnessed many people struggling to explain what they want to do next and why a change makes sense. One of us, in the context of writing a book, has studied a wide variety of major career shifts; the other has worked extensively with organizations and individuals on the use of narrative to bring about positive change. Each of us has been to enough networking events to know that the one we've described here is not unusual. But we've also seen a lot of people in the midst of significant transitions make effective use of contacts and successfully enlist supporters. What we've come to understand is that one factor more than any other makes the difference: the ability to craft a good story.

Why You Need a Story

All of us tell stories about ourselves. Stories define us. To know someone well is to know her story—the experiences that have shaped her, the trials and turning points that have tested her. When we want someone to know us, we share stories of our childhoods, our families, our school years, our first loves, the development of our political views, and so on.

Seldom is a good story so needed, though, as when a major change of professional direction is under way—when we are leaving A without yet having left it and moving toward B without yet having gotten there. In a time of such unsettling transition, telling a compelling story to coworkers, bosses, friends, or family—or strangers in a conference room—inspires belief in our motives, character, and capacity to reach the goals we've set.

Let's be clear: In urging the use of effective narrative, we're not opening the door to tall tales. By "story" we don't mean "something made up to make a bad situation look good." Rather, we're talking about accounts that are deeply true and so engaging that listeners feel they have a stake in our success. This dynamic was lacking in the event described above. Without a story, there was no context to render career facts meaningful, no promise of a third act in which achieving a goal (getting a job, for instance) would resolve the drama.

Creating and telling a story that resonates also helps us believe in ourselves. Most of us experience the transition to a new working life as a time of confusion, loss, insecurity, and uncertainty. We are scared. "Will I look back one day and think this was the best thing that ever happened?" we ask ourselves. "Or will I realize that this was the beginning of the end, that it was all downhill from here?" We oscillate between holding on to the past and embracing the future. Why? We have lost the narrative thread of our professional life. Without a compelling story that lends meaning, unity, and purpose to our lives, we feel lost and rudderless. We need a good story to reassure us that our plans make sense—that, in moving on, we are not discarding everything we have worked so hard to accomplish and selfishly putting family and livelihood at risk. It will give us motivation and help us endure frustration, suffering, and hard work.

A good story, then, is essential for making a successful transition. Yet most of us—like those at the networking event—fail to use the power of storytelling in pursuit of our cause. Or, when we do craft a story, we do it badly. In part, this may be because many of us have forgotten how to tell stories. But even the best storytellers find tales of transition challenging, with their built-in problems and tensions. Not knowing how to resolve these conflicts, we retreat to telling "just the facts."

Your Story Has Inherent Drama

At first glance, it's not obvious why stories of transition should present any problems at all. Almost by definition, they contain the stuff of good narrative. (See the sidebar "Key Elements of a Classic Story" at the end of this article.) The protagonist is you, of course, and what's at stake is your career. Only love, life, and death could be more important. And transition is always about a world that's changed. You've been let go, or you've somehow decided your life doesn't work anymore. Perhaps you've reached an event or insight that represents a point of no return—one that marks the end of the second act, a period of frustration and struggle. In the end, if all goes well, you resolve the tension and uncertainty and embark on a new chapter in your life or career.

Not only do transition stories have all the elements of a classic tale, but they have the most important ones in spades. Notice what moves a story along. It's change, conflict, tension, discontinuity. What hooks us in a movie or novel is the turning point, the break with the past, the fact that the world has changed in some intriguing and fascinating way that will force the protagonist to discover and reveal who he truly is. If those elements are missing, the story will be flat. It will lack what novelist John Gardner called profluence of development—the sense of moving forward, of going somewhere. Transition stories don't have this problem.

Think, for example, of the biblical story of Saint Paul's conversion. In his zeal for Jewish law, Saul had become a violent persecutor of Christians. On the road to Damascus, as the story is told in the New Testament, he was surrounded by light and struck to the ground. A voice from heaven addressed him: "Saul, Saul, why do you persecute me?" He was unable to see; after he changed his mind about Christians, he saw the light, literally. And thus, Saul became Paul, one of the principal architects of Christianity.

What could be more dramatic? Like the Saul-to-Paul saga, most after-the-fact accounts of career change include striking jolts and triggers: palpable moments when things click into place and a desirable option materializes. The scales fall from our eyes, and the right course becomes obvious—or taking the leap suddenly looks easy.

Here's how that turning point took shape for one manager, a 46-year-old information technologist named Lucy Hartman (names in the examples throughout this article have been changed). Lucy was seemingly on a course toward executive management, either at her current company or at a start-up. Being coached, however, revealed to her an attractive alternative. She began to wonder about a future as an organizational-development consultant, but she wasn't quite ready to make that change. She did move to a smaller company, where she felt she could apply everything she had learned in coaching. "By this time, it was clear that I wanted to move on to something different," she said. "But I needed to build more confidence before taking a bigger chance on reinventing myself. So I decided to stay in the high-tech environment, which I knew well, but also to go back to school. I started a master's program in organizational development, thinking it would at least make me a better leader and hoping it would be the impetus for a real makeover." Still, Lucy agonized for months over whether to focus exclusively on school, convinced that it wasn't sane to quit a job without having another one lined up.

Three incidents in quick succession made up her mind. First, she attended a conference on organizational change where she heard industry gurus speak and met other people working in the field. She decided this was clearly the community she wanted to be a part of. Second, her firm went through an acquisition, and the restructuring meant a new position for her, one fraught with political jockeying. Third, as she tells it: "One day my husband just asked me, 'Are you happy?' He said, 'If you are, that's great. But you don't look happy. When I ask how you are, all you ever say is that you're tired.'" His question prompted her to quit her job and work full-time on her master's.

Lucy's story illustrates the importance of turning points. We need them to convince ourselves that our story makes sense, and listeners like them because they spin stories off in exciting new directions. They make listeners lean forward and ask the one question every effective story must elicit: "What happened next?"

The Challenge of the Transition Story

Let's return to that networking event and all the drab stories (actually, nonstories) people told. If transition stories, with their drama and discontinuity, lend themselves so well to vivid telling, why did so many people merely recount the basic facts of their careers and avoid the exciting turning points? Why did most of them try to frame the changes in their lives as incremental, logical extensions of what they were doing before? Why did they fail to play up the narrative twists and turns?

To begin with, it's because they were attempting to tell the story while they were still in the middle of the second act. Look back over Lucy's story, and you'll realize that the turning points she described were not very different from incidents all of us experience daily. They assumed great significance for Lucy only because she made them do so. For most of us, turning points are like Lucy's rather than Saul's; they tend to be much more obvious in the telling than in the living. We must learn to use them to propel our stories forward.

Additionally, stories of transition present a challenge because telling them well involves baring some emotion. You have to let the listener know that something is at stake for you personally. When you're in a job interview or when you are speaking to relative strangers, that is difficult to do.

Another issue that makes life stories (particularly ones about discontinuity) problematic: Not only does a good story require us to trust the listener, but it must also inspire the listener to trust us. A story about life discontinuity raises red flags about the teller's capabilities, dependability, and predictability. Listeners wonder, "Why should I believe you can excel in a new arena when you don't have a track record to point to?" And on a deeper level, even greater suspicions lurk: "Why should I trust that you won't change your mind about this? You changed your mind before, didn't you?"

To tell a life story that emphasizes such juicy elements as transformation and discontinuity is to invite questions about who we are and whether we can be trusted. No one wants to hire somebody who's likely to fly off in an unexpected direction every six months. So we downplay the very things that might make our stories compelling. To earn the listener's trust, we make ourselves appear safe—and dull and unremarkable.

Is there a way to tell a lively story *and* inspire others' confidence? Yes, but it requires a deep understanding of what really makes people believe in what we're saying.

The Struggle for Coherence

All good stories have a characteristic so basic and necessary it's often assumed. That quality is coherence, and it's crucial to life stories of transition.

This was a challenge for Sam Tierman, a former corporate HR executive one of us coached through a career transition. Sam had spent 18 years running HR in a number of good-sized regional banks, but his last three jobs hadn't ended well. He'd been downsized out of one, he'd quit another in frustration, and he'd been fired from the last—which finally led him to realize he had a career problem. While he was energized by the interplay between individuals and organizations, he hated the mundane, administrative aspects of the work. When he had a boss who considered HR a strategic function and who included the HR head at the executive table, he thrived. But when he worked for someone who saw HR as a body shop— "Find the bodies, run the benefits, and keep the government off our back"—Sam hated his work. In his last job, his feelings had been obvious, and a minor problem with some personnel analysis was what did him in. Sam, in fact, had taken this job with high hopes. The CEO who hired him considered HR strategic. Unfortunately, that CEO left and was replaced by one who did not.

As a result, Sam gave up on finding or keeping a boss he could work with in a corporate setting. As do so many frustrated executives, he decided he would prefer to work for a start-up. The problem was that he lacked, on the face of it, any of the experience or qualities wanted by people who found and fund start-ups. It was not obvious how Sam could tell a coherent career story that would bridge the chasm between stodgy overhead departments in banks and the high-energy world of start-ups.

Coherent narratives hang together in ways that feel natural and intuitive. A coherent life story is one that suggests what we all want to believe of ourselves and those we help or hire—that our lives are series of unfolding, linked events that make sense. In other words, the past is related to the present, and from that trajectory, we can glimpse our future.

Coherence is crucial to a life story of transition because it is the characteristic that most generates the listener's trust. If you can make your story of change and reinvention seem coherent, you will have gone far in convincing the listener that the change makes sense for you and is likely to bring success—and that you're a stable, trustworthy person.

As important, you will also have gone far in convincing yourself. Indeed, it's the loss of coherence that makes times of transition so difficult to get through. Think of the cartoon character who's run off the edge of a cliff. Legs still churning like crazy, he doesn't realize he's over the abyss—until he looks down. Each of us in transition feels like that character. Coherence is the solid ground under our feet. Without it, we feel as though we're hanging in midair—and we're afraid that if we look down, we'll plummet to our doom.

Charlotte Linde, a linguist who has studied the importance of coherence in life stories, makes clear in her work
that coherence emerges in large part from continuity
and causality. If we fail to observe these two principles,
we create a sense of incoherence, or, in Linde's words,
the "chilling possibility that one's life is random, acciden-
tal, unmotivated." And what's chilling to us will certainly
be off-putting to those listening to our stories.

Emphasizing Continuity and Causality

Now it becomes understandable why so many speakers
in that networking meeting failed to do more than recite
facts. They were trying to downplay discontinuity; to
gloss over how large a professional jump they wanted to
make; to avoid appearing wayward, lost, and flailing. It
was a misguided strategy, for listeners are particularly
sensitive to lapses of coherence in life stories. They actually *look for* coherence in such stories. Failure to
acknowledge a large degree of change will put off listeners and undermine their trust.

As storytellers, we must deal explicitly with the magni-
tude of change our stories communicate. We can do that
and still inspire trust if we focus on establishing continuity and causality. The following suggestions can help.

**Keep your reasons for change grounded in your
character, in who you are.** There's probably no ratio-
nale for change more compelling than some internal reason, some basic character trait. In its simplest version,
this explanation takes the form of "I discovered I'm good
at that" or "I like that—it gives me real pleasure." This
approach, noted by Linde and found by us in our work to
be extremely useful, allows storytellers to incorporate

learning and self-discovery into life stories. We can try something, learn from the experience, and use that learning to deepen our understanding of what we want. Many turning points can be used in this way. Note that it's not wise to base the reasons for transformation primarily outside ourselves. "I got fired" may be a fact we must explain and incorporate into our stories, but it's rarely recognized as a good justification for seeking whatever we're seeking. External reasons tend to create the impression that we simply accept our fate.

Cite multiple reasons for what you want. You might, for instance, mention both personal and professional grounds for making a change. (Obviously, these must be complementary rather than mutually exclusive or contradictory.) The richer and more varied the reasons compelling you to change, the more comprehensible and acceptable that change will appear. Sam, the former HR executive, was able to cite a number of unusual projects he had worked on, which indicated, though in a big-company context, his ability to think and act entrepreneurially. Additionally, his undergraduate training in electrical engineering and his MBA in finance from a prestigious school were evidence of the technical and analytical bent preferred by the start-ups he knew.

Be sure to point out any explanations that extend back in time. A goal rooted in the past will serve far better than one recently conceived. Your story will need to show why you could not pursue the goal originally, but here, external causes—illness, accident, family problems, being drafted, and so on—can play a leading role.

Reframe your past in light of the change you're seeking to make. This is not to suggest that you hide anything or prevaricate. We all continually rethink and retell our own life stories. We create different versions that focus on or downplay, include or exclude, different aspects of what has happened to us. Some elements of the jobs we've held probably fit well with our change plans and can be used to link our past experiences with the part of our life that we're advancing toward. The key is to dissect those experiences and find the pieces that relate to our current goals. (For advice on how to do this, see the sidebar "Does Your Résumé Tell a Story?" at the end of this article)

Choose a story form that lends itself to your tale of reinvention. Certain forms—love stories, war stories, epics—are as old as narrative itself. There are stories of being tested and stories of being punished. When it comes to describing transition and reinvention, it can be helpful to present the story in a vessel familiar to most listeners. Of the time-honored approaches, two to consider are the maturation (or coming-of-age) plot and the education plot.

The maturation plot was useful to Gary McCarthy, who quit his job as a strategy consultant with no idea of what he would do next. As he told his story at age 35, he looked back over his career and realized he had always responded to social pressure, bending to what others thought was the right thing for him to do. After receiving a negative performance appraisal, he saw that he needed to be his own man. "You'd better be damn sure when you wake up that you're doing what you want to be doing," he said to himself, "as opposed to what you feel you ought to be doing or what somebody else thinks you ought to be doing."

Lucy Hartman's story is a good example of the education plot, which recounts change generated by growing insight and self-understanding. It was a mentor, her executive coach, who let her glimpse a possible new future, and she continued to learn in her master's program and by coaching others. In her version of events, the more she learned about the human side of enterprise, the more she realized her desire to work in and contribute to this area.

All these suggestions are ways to frame the discontinuity in a transition story and provide the coherence that will reassure listeners. They demonstrate that, at your core, the person you were yesterday is the person you are today and the person you will be tomorrow. And they establish that there are good and sufficient causes for change. If you create the sense that your life hangs (and will hang) together, you'll be free to incorporate the dramatic elements of change and turmoil and uncertainty into your story that will make it compelling.

Telling Multiple Stories

We've noted the challenge of crafting a story, complete with dramatic turning points, when the outcome is still far from clear. The truth is, as you embark on a career transition, you will likely find yourself torn among different interests, paths, and priorities. It wouldn't be unusual, for example, for you to work all weekend on a business plan for a start-up, return to your day job on Monday and ask for a transfer to another position or business unit, and then have lunch on Tuesday with a headhunter to explore yet a third option. This is simply the nature of career transition. So how do you reconcile this reality with the need to present a clear, single life story of reinvention, one that implies you know exactly where you're going?

For starters, keep in mind that, in a job interview, you don't establish trust by getting everything off your chest or being completely open about the several possibilities you are exploring. In the early stages of a transition, it is important to identify and actively consider multiple alternatives. But you will explore each option, or type of option, with a different audience.

This means that you must craft different stories for different possible selves (and the various audiences that relate to those selves). Sam chose to focus on start-ups as the result of a process that began with examining his own experience. He realized that he had felt most alive during times he described as "big change fast"—a bankruptcy, a turnaround, and a rapid reorganization. So he developed three stories to support his goal of building a work life around "big change fast": one about the HR contributions he could make on a team at a consulting company that specialized in taking clients through rapid change; one about working for a firm that bought troubled companies and rapidly turned them around; and one about working for a start-up, probably a venture between its first and second, or second and third, rounds of financing. He tested these stories on friends and at networking events and eventually wrangled referrals and job interviews for each kind of job.

The process is not only about keeping options open as long as possible; it's also about learning which ones to pursue most energetically. In Sam's case, what became clear over a number of conversations was that the consulting firms he respected tended not to hire people of his age and credentials unless they had perfectly relevant experience. Neither did opportunities with turnaround firms appear to be panning out. But Sam did make progress toward some start-ups. After one of them engaged him for a series of consulting assignments, he was able to convert that relationship into a job as chief administrative officer. That position, in turn, exposed him to many contacts in the start-up community. Most important, it stamped him as a bona fide member of that world. Having stripped the stodgy corporate aura from his résumé, he eventually became the CEO of a start-up set to commercialize some technology developed by and spun out of a large company. By this point, four full years had elapsed, and Sam had revised his narrative many times, with each step contributing to a more and more coherent story of change.

Just Tell It

Any veteran storyteller will agree that there's no substitute for practicing in front of a live audience. Tell and retell your story; rework it like a draft of an epic novel until the "right" version emerges.

You can practice your stories in many ways and places. Any context will do in which you're likely to be asked, "What can you tell me about yourself?" or "What do you do?" or "What are you looking for?" Start with family and friends. You may even want to designate a small circle of friends and close colleagues, with their knowledge and approval, your "board of advisers." Their primary function would be to listen and react again and again to your evolving stories. Many of the people we have studied or coached through the transition process have created or joined networking groups for just this purpose.

You'll know you've honed your story when it feels both comfortable and true to you. But you cannot get there until you put yourself in front of others—ultimately, in front of strangers—and watch their faces and body language as you speak. For one woman we know, June Prescott, it was not simply that practice made for polished presentation—although her early efforts to explain herself were provisional, even clumsy. (She was attempting a big career change, from academe to Wall Street.) Each time she wrote a cover letter, interviewed, or updated friends and family on her progress, she better defined what was exciting to her; and in each public declaration of her intent to change careers, she committed herself further.

June's experience teaches a final, important lesson about undergoing change. We use stories to reinvent ourselves. June, like Sam, was able to change because she created a story that justified and motivated such a dramatic shift.

This is the role of storytelling in times of personal transition. Getting the story right is critical, as much for motivating ourselves as for enlisting the help of others. Anyone trying to make a change has to work out a story that connects the old and new selves. For it is in a period of change that we often fail, yet most need, to link our past, present, and future into a compelling whole.

Key Elements of a Classic Story

ALL GREAT STORIES, from *Antigone* to *Casablanca* to *Star Wars*, derive their power from several basic characteristics:

- **A protagonist the listener cares about.** The story must be about a person or group whose struggles we can relate to.

- **A catalyst compelling the protagonist to take action.** Somehow the world has changed so that something important is at stake. Typically, the first act of a play is devoted to establishing this fact. It's up to the protagonist to put things right again.

- **Trials and tribulations.** The story's second act commences as obstacles produce frustration, conflict, and drama, and often lead the protagonist to change in an essential way. As in *The Odyssey*, the trials reveal, test, and shape the protagonist's character. Time is spent wandering in the wilderness, far from home.

- **A *turning point*.** This represents a point of no return, which closes the second act. The protagonist can no longer see or do things the same way as before.

- **A *resolution*.** This is the third act, in which the protagonist either succeeds magnificently or fails tragically.

This is the classic beginning-middle-end story structure defined by Aristotle more than 2,300 years ago and used by countless others since. It seems to reflect how the human mind wants to organize reality.

Does Your Résumé Tell a Story?

THOUGH THE TERMS are often used interchangeably, there's a big difference between a curriculum vitae and a résumé.

A CV is an exhaustive and strictly chronological list of facts about your professional life. You may need one, but don't expect it to serve your cause in a period of transition. To the extent it tells a story, that story is constructed wholly in the reader's mind.

If you want to give your credentials narrative shape, use a résumé—and understand that you will almost certainly need more than one version. Each will highlight and interpret your experience differently in light of the job or career alternatives you're exploring.

The process of putting together a résumé is as valuable as the product, because it entails drafting your story. Everything in the résumé must point to one goal—which, of course, is the climax of the story you're telling. Build it in three parts.

First, describe the position you want.

Second, create a bulleted list of experience highlights that clearly demonstrate your ability to do that job. Consider every piece of experience you have (don't forget volunteer work or anything else that might apply), and identify which parts support the story you're telling.

Third, summarize your professional work. This section of your résumé has the appearance of a CV, in reverse chronological order, and includes all the relevant positions you've held; for each job, it shows dates of employment as well as your responsibilities and accomplishments. But these descriptions are couched in the same terms as your experience highlights. In fact, every claim in your highlights section (which supports your overall goal) must be supported by your job summaries.

Follow these steps, and your résumé will tell a coherent story. The work you have done, and the skills and interests you have developed and revealed, will point to a clear and desirable resolution: your stated goal.

Originally published in January 2005
Reprint R0501F

How to Play to Your Strengths

LAURA MORGAN ROBERTS, GRETCHEN
SPREITZER, JANE DUTTON, ROBERT QUINN,
EMILY HEAPHY, AND BRIANNA BARKER

Executive Summary

MOST FEEDBACK ACCENTUATES the negative. During
formal employee evaluations, discussions invariably
focus on "opportunities for improvement," even if the
overall evaluation is laudatory. No wonder most executives—and their direct reports—dread them.

Traditional, corrective feedback has its place, of
course; every organization must filter out failing employees and ensure that everyone performs at an expected
level of competence. But too much emphasis on problem
areas prevents companies from reaping the best from
their people. After all, it's a rare baseball player who is
equally good at every position. Why should a natural
third baseman labor to develop his skills as a right
fielder?

This article presents a tool to help you understand
and leverage your strengths. Called the Reflected Best

Self (RBS) exercise, it offers a unique feedback experience that counterbalances negative input. It allows you to tap into talents you may or may not be aware of and so increase your career potential.

To begin the RBS exercise, you first need to solicit comments from family, friends, colleagues, and teachers, asking them to give specific examples of times in which those strengths were particularly beneficial. Next, you need to search for common themes in the feedback, organizing them in a table to develop a clear picture of your strong suits. Third, you must write a self-portrait—a description of yourself that summarizes and distills the accumulated information. And finally, you need to redesign your personal job description to build on what you're good at.

The RBS exercise will help you discover who you are at the top of your game. Once you're aware of your best self, you can shape the positions you choose to play—both now and in the next phase of your career.

MOST FEEDBACK ACCENTUATES the negative. During formal employee evaluations, discussions invariably focus on "opportunities for improvement," even if the overall evaluation is laudatory. Informally, the sting of criticism lasts longer than the balm of praise. Multiple studies have shown that people pay keen attention to negative information. For example, when asked to recall important emotional events, people remember four negative memories for every positive one. No wonder most executives give and receive performance reviews with all the enthusiasm of a child on the way to the dentist.

Traditional, corrective feedback has its place, of course; every organization must filter out failing employees and ensure that everyone performs at an expected level of competence. Unfortunately, feedback that ferrets out flaws can lead otherwise talented managers to over-invest in shoring up or papering over their perceived weaknesses, or forcing themselves onto an ill-fitting template. Ironically, such a focus on problem areas prevents companies from reaping the best performance from its people. After all, it's a rare baseball player who is equally good at every position. Why should a natural third baseman labor to develop his skills as a right fielder?

The alternative, as the Gallup Organization researchers Marcus Buckingham, Donald Clifton, and others have suggested, is to foster excellence in the third baseman by identifying and harnessing his unique strengths. It is a paradox of human psychology that while people remember criticism, they respond to praise. The former makes them defensive and therefore unlikely to change, while the latter produces confidence and the desire to perform better. Managers who build up their strengths can reach their highest potential. This positive approach does not pretend to ignore or deny the problems that traditional feedback mechanisms identify. Rather, it offers a separate and unique feedback experience that counterbalances negative input. It allows managers to tap into strengths they may or may not be aware of and so contribute more to their organizations.

During the past few years, we have developed a powerful tool to help people understand and leverage their individual talents. Called the Reflected Best Self (RBS) exercise, our method allows managers to develop a sense of their "personal best" in order to increase their future potential. The RBS exercise is but one example of new approaches springing from an area of research called positive organizational scholarship (POS). Just as psychologists know that people respond better to praise than to criticism, organizational behavior scholars are finding that when companies focus on positive attributes such as resilience and trust, they can reap impressive bottom-line returns. (For more on this research, see the insert "The Positive Organization" at the end of this article.) Thousands of executives, as well as tomorrow's leaders enrolled in business schools around the world, have completed the RBS exercise.

In this article, we will walk you through the RBS exercise step-by-step and describe the insights and results it can yield. Before we proceed, however, a few caveats are in order. First, understand that the tool is not designed to stroke your ego; its purpose is to assist you in developing a plan for more effective action. (Without such a plan, you'll keep running in place.) Second, the lessons generated from the RBS exercise can elude you if you don't pay sincere attention to them. If you are too burdened by time pressures and job demands, you may just file the information away and forget about it. To be effective, the exercise requires commitment, diligence, and follow-through. It may even be helpful to have a coach keep you on task. Third, it's important to conduct the RBS exercise at a different time of year than the traditional performance review so that negative feedback from traditional mechanisms doesn't interfere with the results of the exercise.

Used correctly, the RBS exercise can help you tap into unrecognized and unexplored areas of potential. Armed with a constructive, systematic process for gathering and analyzing data about your best self, you can burnish your performance at work.

Step 1
Identify Respondents and Ask for Feedback

The first task in the exercise is to collect feedback from a variety of people inside and outside work. By gathering input from a variety of sources—family members, past and present colleagues, friends, teachers, and so on—you can develop a much broader and richer understanding of yourself than you can from a standard performance evaluation.

As we describe the process of the Reflected Best Self exercise, we will highlight the experience of Robert Duggan (not his real name), whose self-discovery process is typical of the managers we've observed. Having retired from a successful career in the military at a fairly young age and earned an MBA from a top business school, Robert accepted a midlevel management position at an IT services firm. Despite strong credentials and leadership experience, Robert remained stuck in the same position year after year. His performance evaluations were generally good but not strong enough to put him on the high-potential track. Disengaged, frustrated, and disheartened, Robert grew increasingly stressed and disillusioned with his company. His workday felt more and more like an episode of *Survivor*.

Seeking to improve his performance, Robert enrolled in an executive education program and took the RBS exercise. As part of the exercise, Robert gathered feedback from 11 individuals from his past and present who knew him well. He selected a diverse but balanced group—his wife and two other family members, two friends from his MBA program, two colleagues from his time in the army, and four current colleagues.

Robert then asked these individuals to provide information about his strengths, accompanied by specific examples of moments when Robert used those strengths in ways that were meaningful to them, to their families or teams, or to their organizations. Many people—Robert among them—feel uncomfortable asking for exclusively positive feedback, particularly from colleagues. Accustomed to hearing about their strengths and weaknesses simultaneously, many executives imagine any positive feedback will be unrealistic, even false. Some also worry that respondents might construe the request as presumptuous or egotistical. But once managers accept that the exercise will help them improve their performance, they tend to dive in.

Within ten days, Robert received e-mail responses from all 11 people describing specific instances when he had made important contributions—including pushing for high quality under a tight deadline, being inclusive in communicating with a diverse group, and digging for critical information. The answers he received surprised him. As a military veteran and a technical person holding an MBA, Robert rarely yielded to his emotions. But in reading story after story from his respondents, Robert found himself deeply moved—as if he were listening to appreciative speeches at a party thrown in his honor. The stories were also surprisingly convincing. He had more strengths than he knew. (For more on Step 1, refer to the insert "Gathering Feedback.")

Step 2
Recognize Patterns

In this step, Robert searched for common themes among
the feedback, adding to the examples with observations
of his own, then organizing all the input into a table. (To
view parts of Robert's table, see the exhibit "Finding
Common Themes.") Like many who participate in the
RBS exercise, Robert expected that, given the diversity of
respondents, the comments he received would be inconsistent or even competing. Instead, he was struck by
their uniformity. The comments from his wife and family
members were similar to those from his army buddies
and work colleagues. Everyone took note of Robert's
courage under pressure, high ethical standards, perseverance, curiosity, adaptability, respect for diversity, and
team-building skills. Robert suddenly realized that even
his small, unconscious behaviors had made a huge
impression on others. In many cases, he had forgotten
about the specific examples cited until he read the feedback, because his behavior in those situations had felt
like second nature to him.

The RBS exercise confirmed Robert's sense of himself,
but for those who are unaware of their strengths, the
exercise can be truly illuminating. Edward, for example,
was a recently minted MBA executive in an automotive
firm. His colleagues and subordinates were older and
more experienced than he, and he felt uncomfortable
disagreeing with them. But he learned through the RBS
exercise that his peers appreciated his candid alternative
views and respected the diplomatic and respectful manner with which he made his assertions. As a result,
Edward grew bolder in making the case for his ideas,

knowing that his boss and colleagues listened to him, learned from him, and appreciated what he had to say.

Other times, the RBS exercise sheds a more nuanced light on the skills one takes for granted. Beth, for exam-

---

Finding Common Themes

Creating a table helps you make sense of the feedback you collect. By clustering examples, you can more easily compare responses and identify common themes.

Common Theme	Examples Given	Possible Interpretation
Ethics, Values, and Courage	• I take a stand when superiors and peers cross the boundaries of ethical behavior. • I am not afraid to stand up for what I believe in. I confront people who litter or who yell at their kids in public.	• I am at my best when I choose the harder right over the easier wrong. I derive even more satisfaction when I am able to teach others. I am professionally courageous.
Curiosity and Perseverance	• I gave up a promising career in the military to get my MBA. • I investigated and solved a security breach though an innovative approach.	• I like meeting new challenges. I take risks and persevere despite obstacles.
Ability to Build Teams	• In high school, I assembled a team of students that helped improve the school's academic standards. • I am flexible and willing to learn from others, and I give credit where credit is due.	• I thrive when working closely with others.

ple, was a lawyer who negotiated on behalf of nonprofit organizations. Throughout her life, Beth had been told she was a good listener, but her exercise respondents noted that the interactive, empathetic, and insightful manner in which she listened made her particularly effective. The specificity of the feedback encouraged Beth to take the lead in future negotiations that required delicate and diplomatic communications.

For naturally analytical people, the analysis portion of the exercise serves both to integrate the feedback and develop a larger picture of their capabilities. Janet, an engineer, thought she could study her feedback as she would a technical drawing of a suspension bridge. She saw her "reflected best self" as something to interrogate and improve. But as she read the remarks from family, friends, and colleagues, she saw herself in a broader and more human context. Over time, the stories she read about her enthusiasm and love of design helped her rethink her career path toward more managerial roles in which she might lead and motivate others.

Step 3
Compose Your Self-Portrait

The next step is to write a description of yourself that summarizes and distills the accumulated information. The description should weave themes from the feedback together with your self-observations into a composite of who you are at your best. The self-portrait is not designed to be a complete psychological and cognitive profile. Rather, it should be an insightful image that you can use as a reminder of your previous contributions and as a guide for future action. The portrait itself should not be a set of bullet points but rather a prose composition beginning with the phrase, "When I am at my best, I . . ." The process of writing out a two- to four-paragraph narrative cements the image of your best self in your consciousness. The narrative form also helps you draw connections between the themes in your life that may previously have seemed disjointed or unrelated. Composing the portrait takes time and demands careful consideration, but at the end of this process, you should come away with a rejuvenated image of who you are.

In developing his self-portrait, Robert drew on the actual words that others used to describe him, rounding out the picture with his own sense of himself at his best. He excised competencies that felt off the mark. This didn't mean he discounted them, but he wanted to assure that the overall portrait felt authentic and powerful. "When I am at my best," Robert wrote,

> *I stand by my values and can get others to understand why doing so is important. I choose the harder right over the easier wrong. I enjoy setting an example. When I am in learning mode and am curious and passionate about a project, I can work intensely and untiringly. I enjoy taking things on that others might be afraid of or see as too difficult. I'm able to set limits and find alternatives when a current approach is not working. I don't always assume that I am right or know best, which engenders respect from others. I try to empower and give credit to others. I am tolerant and open to differences.*

As Robert developed his portrait, he began to understand why he hadn't performed his best at work: He lacked a sense of mission. In the army, he drew satisfaction from the knowledge that the safety of the men and women he led, as well as the nation he served, depended on the quality of his work. He enjoyed the sense of team-work and variety of problems to be solved. But as an IT manager in charge of routine maintenance on new hard-ware products, he felt bored and isolated from other people.

The portrait-writing process also helped Robert create a more vivid and elaborate sense of what psychologists would call his "possible self"—not just the person he is in his day-to-day job but the person he might be in com-pletely different contexts. Organizational researchers have shown that when we develop a sense of our best possible self, we are better able make positive changes in our lives.

Step 4
Redesign Your Job

Having pinpointed his strengths, Robert's next step was to redesign his personal job description to build on what he was good at. Given the fact that routine maintenance work left him cold, Robert's challenge was to create a better fit between his work and his best self. Like most RBS participants, Robert found that the strengths the exercise identified could be put into play in his current position. This involved making small changes in the way he worked, in the composition of his team, and in the way he spent his time. (Most jobs have degrees of free-dom in all three of these areas; the trick is operating within the fixed constraints of your job to redesign work at the margins, allowing you to better play to your strengths.)

Robert began by scheduling meetings with systems designers and engineers who told him they were having trouble getting timely information flowing between their groups and Robert's maintenance team. If communication improved, Robert believed, new products would not continue to be saddled with the serious and costly maintenance issues seen in the past. Armed with a carefully documented history of those maintenance problems as well as a new understanding of his naturally analytical and creative team-building skills, Robert began meeting regularly with the designers and engineers to brainstorm better ways to prevent problems with new products. The meetings satisfied two of Robert's deepest best-self needs: He was interacting with more people at work, and he was actively learning about systems design and engineering.

Robert's efforts did not go unnoticed. Key executives remarked on his initiative and his ability to collaborate across functions, as well as on the critical role he played in making new products more reliable. They also saw how he gave credit to others. In less than nine months, Robert's hard work paid off, and he was promoted to program manager. In addition to receiving more pay and higher visibility, Robert enjoyed his work more. His passion was reignited; he felt intensely alive and authentic. Whenever he felt down or lacking in energy, he reread the original e-mail feedback he had received. In difficult situations, the e-mail messages helped him feel more resilient.

Robert was able to leverage his strengths to perform better, but there are cases in which RBS findings conflict with the realities of a person's job. This was true for James, a sales executive who told us he was "in a world of hurt" over his work situation. Unable to meet his ambitious sales goals, tired of flying around the globe to fight fires, his family life on the verge of collapse, James had suffered enough. The RBS exercise revealed that James was at his best when managing people and leading change, but these natural skills did not and could not come into play in his current job. Not long after he did the exercise, he quit his high-stress position and started his own successful company.

Other times, the findings help managers aim for undreamed-of positions in their own organizations. Sarah, a high-level administrator at a university, shared her best-self portrait with key colleagues, asking them to help her identify ways to better exploit her strengths and talents. They suggested that she would be an ideal candidate for a new executive position. Previously, she would never have considered applying for the job, believing herself unqualified. To her surprise, she handily beat out the other candidates.

Beyond Good Enough

We have noted that while people remember criticism, awareness of faults doesn't necessarily translate into better performance. Based on that understanding, the RBS exercise helps you remember your strengths—and construct a plan to build on them. Knowing your strengths also offers you a better understanding of how to deal with your weaknesses—and helps you gain the confidence you need to address them. It allows you to say, "I'm great at leading but lousy at numbers. So rather than teach me remedial math, get me a good finance partner." It also allows you to be clearer in addressing your areas of weakness as a manager. When Tim, a financial services executive, received feedback that he was a great listener and coach, he also became more aware that he had a tendency to spend too much time being a cheerleader and too little time keeping his employees to task. Susan, a senior advertising executive, had the opposite problem: While her feedback lauded her results-oriented management approach, she wanted to be sure that she hadn't missed opportunities to give her employees the space to learn and make mistakes.

In the end, the strength-based orientation of the RBS exercise helps you get past the "good enough" bar. Once you discover who you are at the top of your game, you can use your strengths to better shape the positions you choose to play—both now and in the next phase of your career.

The Positive Organization

POSITIVE ORGANIZATIONAL SCHOLARSHIP (POS) is an area of organizational behavior research that focuses on the positive dynamics (such as strength, resilience, vitality, trust, and so on) that lead to positive effects (like improved productivity and performance) in individuals and organizations. The word "positive" refers to the discipline's affirmative bias, "organizational" focuses on the processes and conditions that occur in group contexts, and "scholarship" reflects the rigor, theory, scientific procedures, and precise definition in which the approach is grounded.

The premise of POS research is that by understanding the drivers of positive behavior in the workplace, organizations can rise to new levels of achievement. For example, research by Marcial Losada and Emily Heaphy at the University of Michigan suggests that when individuals or teams hear five positive comments to every negative one, they unleash a level of positive energy that fuels higher levels of individual and group performance. Kim Cameron, a POS researcher, has demonstrated how this positive approach has helped the workers at Rocky Flats, a nuclear site in Colorado, tackle difficult and dangerous work in record time. Begun in 1995 and estimated to take 70 years and $36 billion, the Rocky Flats cleanup project is now slated for completion in ten years, with a price tag of less than $7 billion. Kaiser-Hill, the company in charge of the cleanup, replaced a culture of denial with one that fostered employee flexibility and celebrated achievements. The result was that employees developed new procedures that were fast, smart, and safe.

POS does not adopt one particular theory or framework but draws from the full spectrum of organizational theories to explain and predict high performance. To that end, a core part of the POS mission is to create cases, tools, and assessments that can help organizations improve their practices. The Reflected Best Self exercise is just one example of the kinds of practice tools available from POS. (For more information about POS, see the University of Michigan's Web site at www.bus .umich.edu/positive/.)

Gathering Feedback

A CRITICAL STEP in the Reflected Best Self exercise involves soliciting feedback from family, friends, teachers, and colleagues. E-mail is an effective way of doing this, not only because it's comfortable and fast but also because it's easy to cut and paste responses into an analysis table such as the one in the main body of this article.

Below is the feedback Robert, a manager we observed, received from a current colleague and from a former coworker in the army.

From: Amy Chen
To: Robert Duggan
Subject: Re: Request for feedback
Dear Robert,

One of the greatest ways that you add value is that you stand for doing the right thing. For example, I think of the time that we were behind on a project for a major client and quality began to slip. You called a meeting and suggested that we had a choice: We could either pull a C by satisfying the basic requirements, or we could pull an A by doing excellent work. You reminded us that we could contribute to a better outcome. In the end, we met our deadline, and the client was very happy with the result.

From: Mike Bruno
To: Robert Duggan
Subject: Re: Request for feedback

One of the greatest ways you add value is that you persist in the face of adversity. I remember the time that we were both leading troops under tight security. We were getting conflicting information from the ground and from headquarters. You pushed to get the ground and HQ folks to talk to each other despite the tight time pressure. That information saved all of our lives. You never lost your calm, and you never stopped expecting or demanding the best from everyone involved.

Originally published in January 2005
Reprint R0501G

Do Your Commitments Match Your Convictions?

DONALD N. SULL AND DOMINIC HOULDER

Executive Summary

HOW MANY OF US KEEP PACE day to day, upholding our obligations to our bosses, families, and the community, even as our overall satisfaction with work and quality of life decline? And yet, our common response to the situation is: "I'm too busy to do anything about it now." Unfortunately, unless a personal or professional crisis strikes, very few of us step back, take stock of our day-to-day actions, and make a change.

In this article, London Business School strategy professors Donald Sull and Dominic Houlder examine the reasons why a gap often exists between the things we value most and the ways we actually spend our time, money, and attention. They also suggest a practical approach to managing the gap. The framework they propose is based on their study of *organizational* commitments—the investments, promises, and contracts made today that bind companies to a future course of action. Such commitments can prevent organizations from responding effectively to change.

A similar logic applies to *personal* commitments—the day-to-day decisions we make about how we allocate our precious resources. These decisions are individually small and, therefore, easy to lose sight of. When we do, a gap can develop between our commitments and our convictions.

Sull and Houlder make no value judgments about the *content* of personal commitments; they've devised a somewhat dispassionate tool to help you take a thorough inventory of what matters to you most. It involves listing your most important values and assigning to each a percentage of your annual salary, the hours out of your week, and the amount of energy you devote. Using this exercise, you should be able to identify big gaps—stated values that receive little or none of your scarce resources or a single value that sucks a disproportionate share of resources—and change your allocations accordingly.

W E ALL HOLD CERTAIN THINGS DEAR—professional achievement, for example, or family life, or financial security. But when we step back and take stock of our day-to-day actions, we may notice a gap between the things we value most and the way we actually spend our time, money, and attention. It may be a crevice or a chasm, but, in either case, the gap raises questions about how we manage the differences between our professed values and our actual behavior.

Consider the case of Nick, the CEO of a health care products company. (The identities of all the individuals discussed in this article have been disguised to protect their confidentiality.) He turned the organization around after it was taken private by a leveraged buyout firm and has a successful managerial track record in a range of blue-chip and entrepreneurial companies. He is highly regarded by the private-equity investors who own his parent company. But there is a huge gap between what Nick cares about and what he is actually doing. One of the best times in his life, he told us, was when he and his wife took sabbaticals and volunteered for a year with an organization that helps immigrants—a cause that matters greatly to Nick, as the son of immigrants. He misses the time he and his wife spent together that year. "These days, given our schedules, we're lucky to spend more than one weekend a month together," he says. Nick also questions his professional impact. "At 50, I know I have five—maybe ten—good work years left," he says. "But I'm dribbling my life away working in a business that I'm not passionate about and that may or may not make me rich."

Nick is considering several career options. He could take a different CEO job; headhunters do call with offers. If his company were sold at the right price, he could retire early. He could teach at a business school. Or maybe he could work full-time at the nonprofit where he and his wife volunteered. Although Nick feels dissatisfied most days, he believes that any change must wait until he completes a major product launch at work and perhaps until he sees what happens with his equity. He says he is way too busy to do anything right now about the gap between his values and his working life. He's been "too busy" for several years running.

Perhaps your first instinct is to give Nick a thorough shaking. But the truth is, many successful people feel a similar disconnect between their daily activities and their deepest desires—and a similar inability to do anything about it. We became interested in that disconnect almost by accident. Since 1997, we have been teaching a course at London Business School on leading strategic transformations in organizations. The conceptual cornerstone of the course is commitments—the investments, public promises, contracts, and so on that bind an organization to a particular way of doing things. The course, and the research that underlies it, analyzes how historical commitments can create inertia that prevents organizations from responding effectively to changes in the competitive environment. It also explores how managers can commit to new business opportunities and thereby transform their companies.

Over the years, many of our midcareer and executive students borrowed the course's framework of commitments, inertia, and transformation and used it to think systematically about their personal and professional commitments. This happened enough times, and with enough interesting results, that we incorporated into the course a session on managing *personal* commitments. It even includes a computer-based exercise that lets students simulate personal commitments and track what kind of outcomes they may create—think the Sims discover the meaning of life. In the following pages, we'll take a closer look at this framework and describe how it can help midlife and other managers in their quest to narrow the gap between their deeply held values and their everyday activities. Let us be clear, though: We can't—and won't—try to tell you what the *content* of your personal commitments should be. We won't suggest that dedicating yourself to social service is better than making partner. Both are laudable goals. We do

hope to help you improve the *process* ᵗ
age your personal commitments, wh⸍

Defining Commitments

First, let's define our terms and illustrate ⸜
business domain. Managerial commitments are aᵥ
taken in the present that bind an organization to a
future course. When most people think of managerial
commitments, they immediately call to mind dramatic
actions—Boeing betting the company on the 777, for
example, or Oracle acquiring PeopleSoft to build its position in applications software. In the corporate world,
executives manage such commitments systematically.
No responsible CEO would launch a new product or a
make a major acquisition without first conducting
methodical research and tracking progress against quan-
tifiable goals. This is Business 101. Yet the most binding
commitments in business are often so mundane as to be
almost invisible. A company's ongoing investments in
refining and extending an existing technology, for example, can cumulatively lock it onto a technological trajectory from which it is hard to escape. An organization
that concentrates its sales efforts on its key customers
can become dependent on those clients, limiting the
firm's freedom to pursue other clients and other business
options. Taken together, these kinds of mundane commitments can prove as binding as the big bets, yet they
rarely receive the same level of scrutiny from managers.

A similar logic applies in our personal lives, where our
most binding commitments are frequently the result of
day-to-day decisions too small to attract our attention.
There are exceptions, of course. Individuals periodically
make dramatic commitments, such as changing jobs or

g married. And people who choose certain public-
vice careers, such as the military and law enforce-
ment, may make the ultimate commitment by giving
their life to a cause they believe in. For the rest of us,
however, our most important commitments are the
result of mundane decisions we make about how to allocate our money, time, and energy. Because these decisions are individually small, it is easy to lose sight of
them, and when we do, a gap can grow between what we
value and what we do.

Mind the Gap

The first step in managing your commitments is to take
a quick inventory of what matters to you. (For a helpful
work sheet, see the exhibit "Taking Stock.") You probably have at least a vague sense of what you value most,
but it's important to clarify those themes from time to
time. This exercise lets you check whether you are
putting your money (and your time and energy) where
your mouth is. A systematic inventory of where your
money, time, and energy are going often reveals surprising gaps.

Taking Stock

What Matters to Me	Money	Time	Energy
Other			

Using our work sheet, list the things that matter most to you in the first column. A few tips: It's crucial that you avoid overly vague nouns, such as "money" or "family," and instead use more specific gerunds and phrases. "Money," for example, might be articulated as "providing financial security for my family," "earning enough to retire early," or "making more than my business school section-mates." It's worth spending the time to get the language right. "Children," for example, might be broken out into a few more specific values, such as "raising well-educated, morally responsible children" or "enjoying time hanging out with my kids." These are two different values that have distinct implications for how much time you spend with your children and what activities you do with them. If you wrote the former, you might value spending time together on community service; if you wrote the latter, you might want to spend more time together at the beach. Don't be afraid to jot down a value, scratch it out if it doesn't sound quite right, and try again until it does. There is no "right" number of values, but most people find that it takes at least five to cover the multiple dimensions of their lives (for instance, professional, family, social, religious, and individual). If the number creeps beyond ten, you're probably not focusing on the highest priority values or the most critical ones. You might want to ask your spouse or partner to do this stage of the exercise, too. You can then compare notes and explore the significance of any differences you have in what you value most. Finally, it's important to write what you honestly value rather than censoring yourself or imposing judgments about whether you should want something or not. This is not an exercise in what you (or others) *think* you should value but in what *really* matters to you.

The second step is to look closely at how committed you are, practically speaking, to the items listed in the first column. The evidence here will not be in any dramatic actions you may have taken. Such momentous events, you will recall, are comparatively rare in personal life, as they are in business. Rather, the evidence will be in the smaller, more mundane commitments we all routinely make that can collectively lock us on a course of action. You can make the exercise concrete by taking stock of whether your daily investments of money, time, and energy are aligned with your values. Let us look at each category in turn.

MONEY

Over the past year, how much money have you spent on each of the values you listed? To answer this question, you can draw on the data you collect for tax purposes. "Dining out," for instance, may be a line item in your Intuit spreadsheet that jibes nicely with the value "spending time with friends." A word of warning, though: You will have to make some judgment calls. Your personal budget categories are unlikely to map directly to the values you listed. Sometimes they will not correlate at all, and the expenditures should be listed in a miscellaneous "other" category. Other times, your personal spending will map to your values in ways that aren't obvious. By taking a big mortgage on an expensive house in a tony neighborhood, for example, you also buy access to good public schools for your children. Your expenditures may correspond to more than one value, so you may want to split them across several values. You may also find that much of your money is allocated to long-term, fixed investments—a mortgage or a retirement savings account, for instance. You may prefer to assess only your discretionary spending—such as the amount you spend on memberships to health clubs or golf clubs—and leave a review of long-term investments for another time. Or you may discover that your fixed expenses—for instance, the amount you're spending on your summer home in Nantucket—are what most need to be reviewed. (By reducing your fixed costs, you also reduce the effort required to cover them, freeing up time and energy to pursue other alternatives.)

However you resolve these accounting issues, the next step is to convert the expenditures into a percentage of your household income and plot the percentages against your ranked values. (For a sample, see the exhibit "What Matters Most: A Work Sheet") Do the most important values get the most money? If not, there is evidence of a gap between values and commitments.

TIME

Many people find themselves running short of time more often than they run out of money. Time is a scarce resource and one that inevitably gets depleted. By contrast, cash can increase over time if returns on investment exceed the cost of capital. In the past week, what have you done with your approximately 112 waking hours? Again, consider the values you listed, and try to map last week's hours against them. (If last week was atypical, pick the most recent week that you find representative.) As with your money, allocate only those hours that clearly support your stated values, and use the "other" category to account for the difference between total waking hours and those explicitly accounted for in your analysis. Everyone needs some downtime, of course,

What Matters Most: A Work Sheet

Ann Montgomery is a management consultant who has been feeling some incongruity between what she values and what she actually does day to day. She used this work sheet to take inventory of her situation. She listed her values in column one and assessed how much money, time, and energy she spends on each. The percentages listed in column two represent the portions of Ann's household income that support each of her values. The hours noted in column three represent the time Ann allocates, out of total waking hours in a week, to support her stated values. And the entries in column four denote the quality of the physical and mental energy Ann devotes to her values. Values receiving her peak attention get a "+." Values receiving her attention when she's less energetic get a "–".

What Matters to Me	Money	Time	Energy
Raising healthy, balanced kids; spending mostly harmonious time with family	35% mortgage, utilities, and home maintenance 8% trombone lessons, soccer camp, orthodontia 12% variable expenses—bottles of merlot, food at Trader Joe's	15 hours "routine"—being a taxi service, cleaning up after kids, monitoring chores	–/+
		5 hours nagging and pestering kids	–
		5 hours "quality"—having meaningful parent-child conversations, helping with homework	+
Doing interesting, useful work; gaining recognition		60 hours	+

What Matters to Me	Money	Time	Energy
Saving for retirement and kids' college funds; hedging against job loss	33%	15 minutes worrying about Fidelity statement 15 minutes fantasizing about Nasdaq at 10,000	– ++
Spending time on activities that recharge my batteries (reading, writing, exercising, one-on-one time with friends, and vices I'm not going to admit to)	Not much—gym fees, books, merlot, occasional dinners out, treats	5 hours exercising 5 hours reading 0 hours writing	+ – –
Maintaining close relationships—Alex (spouse), Mom, siblings, friends		2 to 5 hours	–/+
Contributing to the church—community service as well as money	2%	0 hours on community service	
Other	10% (darned if I know)	5 to 10 hours watching TV (worse during playoffs), drinking merlot, reading blogs and other stuff online	+

so you may want to include a value like "recharging my mental batteries." But also ask yourself, at what point does spending the afternoon watching college football on TV move beyond healthy rejuvenation and into the realm of wasting precious time? (Even reasonable couples may disagree on this one.) Are you dedicating the most hours to the activities that are of highest value to you? Was there a lot of time you could not account for—time that was not being used to ends that you care about?

ENERGY

Physical, emotional, and mental energy is another scarce resource and, like time, one that decreases with age. An hour spent on an activity when we are fresh and fully present in the moment represents a greater commitment than an hour spent when we are exhausted and distracted. Do the hours you spend with your partner, for example, generally come at the tail end of a 12-hour day and a six-day week? Was your mind plotting Monday's PowerPoint presentation during church or synagogue? On the work sheet, denote those values that, on average, receive your peak attention with a "+" and those that tend to get your least energetic focus with a "−."

Why the Gap?

Once you've filled in the work sheet as we've described, you should end up with a fair analysis of the alignment between what you value and how you commit your money, time, and energy. The basic idea is to identify big gaps—stated values that receive little or none of your scarce resources or a single value that sucks a disproportionate share of money, time, and energy from other values. If your values and your day-to-day commitments are closely aligned, we congratulate you: Many people find it difficult to strike and consistently maintain this balance. Gaps between your commitments and your convictions can develop and widen with time. Understanding how these gaps can emerge is helpful in preventing them from growing too large.

Sometimes the gap results from a reluctance to commit time, energy, or money to what we value. A professional or personal failure, for instance, may shake your confidence and leave you gun-shy about making new commitments. Or perhaps you just have an innate, Peter Pan–like desire to remain in the world of potentiality for as long as possible. Of course, there are times when keeping your options open makes perfect sense. Young adults, for example, experiment with alternative careers, lifestyles, values, and relationships—which is often painful for parents to watch, generally embarrassing in retrospect, but actually a prudent discovery process.

A much more common reason for the gap is that people are entangled in commitments they made in the past. We have observed an analogous phenomenon in corporate strategy. We use the phrase "active inertia" to describe managers' tendency to respond to even the most dramatic changes in their competitive environment by relying on and accelerating activities that worked in the past. Like the driver of a car with its wheels stuck in the mud, executives notice a change in the environment and step on the gas. Ultimately, they end up digging their organizations deeper into the quagmire. The ruts that lock people into active inertia are the very commitments that led to their past successes but that have now hardened: Strategic frames become blinders, selected processes lapse into routines, relation-ships turn into shackles, resources become millstones, and once vibrant values ossify into dogmas.

Many of us are bound by personal commitments we willingly made in the past that no longer fit. They deplete our time, money, and energy and limit our freedom even if the commitments are no longer aligned with what we currently value. Katherine, the chief executive of a mid-size nonprofit company, received an offer to run a private firm. After 20 years in social service, Katherine was attracted by the new challenge as well as the generous health care and pension package, the company car, and the higher salary, which would come in handy as she and her husband put three children through college. In the past, Katherine had derided people who joined the for-profit world as sellouts. She and her husband, a political activist and community organizer, had consciously avoided what they considered the trappings of material life, including flashy cars, elaborate home renovations, and expensive vacations. Katherine's husband was livid when she broached the subject of taking the job, remind-ing her of what their friends would say. (Her husband's idealism was what had attracted Katherine to him in the first place.) Katherine's children, who had unsuccessfully pestered her for years to buy them iPods and PlaySta-tions, accused her of hypocrisy. Although Katherine craved the financial security and new challenge, she felt trapped in a web of commitments she herself had woven.

Some of us experience "commitment creep." We often commit ourselves without really thinking about what we are taking on. It is very easy to say yes to new commit-ments without reflecting on the long-term costs of hon-oring the implied promises or the potential conflicts that may develop with existing commitments. Overcommit-ment is the bane of people who face many good options.

Consider Hannah, a successful New York entrepreneur, who promised to spend more time with her London-based partner. Around the same time, she also received an offer from a large West Coast competitor to buy her start-up company at a juicy valuation. The deal was structured as a five-year earn-out, however, and required Hannah to move to San Francisco to run the combined business. The net result is that she is spending even more time airborne, torn between two major, conflicting commitments she made simultaneously.

The implicit nature of many professional and personal commitments also causes them to sneak up on us unnoticed. Relatively few personal commitments—marriage or religious vows among them—are explicit and public. Recall Nick, the health care CEO described earlier. His major commitment is not contractual; he has never signed an employment agreement. Rather, his sense of obligation arises from the implicit promises he made to Jerry, his company's chairman and principal investor. Nick has worked in senior roles in two of the companies Jerry bought. For more than a decade, Nick has been reinforcing an unspoken commitment to act as Jerry's right-hand man, which has now left him feeling trapped. His reputation, identity, and stock options are as much at stake as if his commitment had been formalized.

Creeping commitments often seem especially binding because they lack the explicit boundaries and exit clauses common to legal documents. Anything you do to honor a creeping commitment will be understood as a reinforcement of an earlier promise or historical commitment—whether that is your intention or not.

Other people's expectations can also prevent us from committing our time, money, and energy to what matters most to us. Many of us measure our success against external benchmarks. Some of us remain prisoners of expectations set by our parents, long after we have left home. From childhood on, "success" means pleasing those who confer grades, jobs, prestige, and promotions. Well into adulthood, through college and graduate school, success remains a function of the esteem we receive from our peers, professors, and recruiters. In the corporate world, practices such as formal project reviews, 360-degree feedback, and annual appraisals increase our dependence on others' assessments of us.

This is fine, unless our values begin to diverge from those of our colleagues. When Ravi joined a Wall Street investment bank just out of college, for example, he cultivated a reputation for being the first in, the last out, and the hardest worker in the hours between. He relished the nickname his colleagues gave him—"the Marine." But after the birth of his first child, he wanted to spend more time with his family, which baffled his colleagues. To Ravi, it was simple: He wanted to continue to be praised for his work ethic, but he also wanted to spend more time at home. By relying on others for validation and praise, Ravi relinquished to them the power to set his priorities. As he discovered, handing the keys to others can be a problem if they're driving someplace you no longer want to go.

Moreover, some values generate less positive reinforcement than others and, as a result, tend to attract fewer resources. Consider the case of Ian, a successful director at a global management-consulting firm. During his 12 years at the company, he moved quickly through the ranks of consultant, manager, partner, and director, garnering a string of exceptional performance reviews along the way. Although Ian highly valued the hours he spent with his family, he found that most of his time and energy were devoted to serving clients, developing junior consultants, and building the firm. When Ian examined the source of this discrepancy (ever the consultant, he used a fish-bone diagram), he discovered that he had become addicted to the positive reinforcement he was getting at work—which his home life couldn't match. At the office, he explained, "my colleagues and clients respect me, and my reviews are glowing. At home, I'm lucky to get a sullen grumble from my teenage daughter and an exhausted kiss from my wife when she gets home from work." Following the principle that "what gets measured gets done," Ian began tracking the hours he spent each week with his wife and daughter and comparing his performance week after week. Ian was pleasantly surprised to find that this simple exercise focused his attention on the hours he spent at home, and the weekly comparison provided a gentle hint that he need to do more of it.

Our historical success in meeting commitments breeds the expectation—in our bosses, colleagues, friends, and family—that we will deliver more of the same. Look at Lee, a corporate tax attorney specializing in the energy industry, who is at the top of her profession. She chairs prestigious committees, publishes in leading journals, and attracts high-profile clients who want her advice on thorny issues. Lee has always loved a professional challenge—in fact, her desire to seek out and solve the hard problems has driven her success. But after 25 years in the field, Lee told us, she had become increasingly bored with her work and longed for the intellectual excitement that characterized the early part of her career. She was reluctant, however, to scale back her lifestyle. Perhaps more important, the prospect of tackling a completely new endeavor—at age 50, no less—seemed daunting to her. "I almost wish I hadn't been so successful in law," she told us, "because then I wouldn't

feel like I had so much to lose if I fell flat on my face trying something new."

The penny dropped at her 25th law school reunion.
One-hundred or so of her contemporaries were all
benchmarking themselves against one another. The
inevitable success stories—Lee was telling them, too—
were like spells that she now wanted to break. She realized she was feeling unfulfilled in part because of the
company she was keeping: She worked all day with the
lawyers and staffers in her firm. And because much of
her time outside work was spent on professional service,
she associated with many of the same attorneys on
evenings and weekends. During her reunion, Lee recognized that her concerns about maintaining her current
lifestyle had a lot to do with her wanting to keep up with
her peers. To make a change, Lee cultivated friendships
with acquaintances outside her immediate circle who
sympathized with her aspiration to do something new
and had themselves made major career shifts. She also
cut in half the amount of time she spent attending professional conferences.

Changing Course

Most people who undertake the self-exploration process
we're describing here find that it's relatively easy to identify their own values, somewhat more difficult to analyze
the gap between their values and the way they actually
live, and harder still to analyze the reasons for this gap.
But the hardest task of all is doing something about
closing the gap. As we know from organizational life,
change is very easy to talk about and extremely difficult
to pull off. The force of inertia is every bit as powerful in
our personal lives as it is in most organizations.

The most common catalyst for serious change is a personal or professional crisis, such as the death of a loved one, a personal illness, a business failure, the loss of a job, or a divorce. No one wishes for crises; they drain not just money, time, and energy but often health, confidence and reputation. But crises do push some people to deliberately reexamine their commitments.

Annette was an independent consultant who worked within a network. Although she was putting in more and more hours, she found that she was spending less and less time on projects that really engaged her imagination and advanced her skills. She was trapped by layers of old commitments, some of which had crept up on her unnoticed. Never wanting to disappoint a client, she invariably delivered excellent work, on time. Her clients and colleagues expected more and more of the same. Years of professional success had left Annette with little freedom to devote herself to the things she really cared about.

Then her mother was diagnosed with terminal cancer, and Annette's priorities changed. At the top of her list was ensuring that her mother got the best possible care. Next was spending quality time with her mother in her final months. Further down the list were her commitments to clients and associates; in many cases, those commitments had to be abandoned. Annette's mother's illness lasted for six months and, like any crisis, consumed considerable time, energy, and money. But it also created advantages both obvious and unforeseen. Specifically:

Crises force people to figure out what really matters. In the end, all crises are reminders that we are not omnipotent or immortal and that we cannot afford to ignore the things that really matter to us. Her mother's illness and death sent a message to Annette: She had to make the most of her own life. That meant committing herself only to those professional projects she found interesting and challenging—not entering into the same kinds of engagements with the same kinds of clients using the same kinds of PowerPoint presentations where only the names change. It also meant spending more time with the people who mattered to her most, including her equally harried partner and her estranged father.

Crises force people to make choices. While some people fail to commit because they feel trapped by promises they've already made, others simply avoid making commitments altogether. A crisis will often demolish our commitment-avoidance strategies. The loss of a job, or an unexpected denial of promotion, can be the catalyst for exploring what we really want to make of our working lives.

Crises can nullify outdated commitments. A crisis in one's personal life is analogous to a force majeure contract clause in a legal document—all previous promises are nullified because of unanticipated or uncontrollable events. The people to whom Annette had previously committed her time and energy, for instance, understood that caring for her mother took precedence over earlier claims on Annette's resources. The slate was clean.

Crises prompt people to clear their diaries. During the six months that Annette was home caring for her mother, she had handed over most of her clients to colleagues, leaving her with a largely empty calendar. That allowed her to rebuild her professional life step by step, taking on new commitments.

Crises help to break the cycle of success. We noted earlier that many successful people feel trapped by their very success. A failure in the workplace, while undoubtedly painful, can also be liberating. Once you and the people around you see that you failed, but that the failure neither killed you nor destroyed your many strengths, it becomes easier to change direction and take on new challenges. When Annette returned to the workplace and began to remake her commitments, she focused on creative and stretch assignments rather than leaning on old ways of doing things.

It's harder (and braver) to make new commitments and rethink old ones when we are not facing a crisis. Which is why time-outs—sabbaticals, executive education courses, or any other catalyst for breaking the thread of a narrative—are so important. Such breaks confer some of the benefits of a crisis—particularly some time to reflect, an excuse to break old commitments, and a chance to clear the diary—without exacting the high costs. That being said, it would be wrong to suggest that changing direction is easy, even if you're reasonably certain about where you want to go. People tend to encounter the following pitfalls when attempting to remake their commitments.

THE GREAT LEAP FORWARD

Some people end up making unrealistic commitments that are bound to fail—great leaps that cannot be made. These commitments can be very enticing; they're novel and exciting for a while. But they are also very risky. Such commitments can provide an excuse for failing to make or keep more mundane commitments. Members of Alcoholics Anonymous, for instance, are discouraged from pledging that they will never drink again; they are

encouraged to take it one day at a time. Or consider
Maria, a Brazilian who received her undergraduate and
MBA degrees in the United States and stayed to work as
a marketing executive in a large consumer goods company in the Midwest. After more than 15 years in the
States, she was anxious to spend more time with her
aging parents in Sao Paulo. She quit her job and moved
to Brazil without lining up a new position. Although she
enjoyed spending more time with her parents, she was
deeply frustrated by her inability to find a position of
comparable responsibility with a world-class company.
And she missed the United States and her friends more
than she had imagined. Two companies and 18 months
later, Maria decided to return to the United States and
concluded that she would have been better served by
taking a one-year posting in Brazil with a multinational
to test the waters professionally and personally.

THE GO-IT-ALONE FALLACY

Remaking historical commitments is not a solo sport;
after all, these are promises others rely on. Social organizations—families, churches, companies, and communities, for instance—are held together by the promises
embedded in individual members' commitments. Undoing these commitments can disrupt organizations and
undermine individuals' credibility. As the world changes
around us or as our values evolve, we need to renegotiate
existing commitments with those who would be affected
by these changes, not try to make unilateral moves. For
example, Susan, a high-powered London-based executive, wants to scale back her professional obligations to
spend more time with her preschool-aged children. To
do so, she would need to talk with her boss and her col-

leagues about how to reduce and restructure her work-load. Even more daunting, in Susan's eyes, is the prospect of discussing with her husband, Donald, how this change in commitments would affect their family and financial responsibilities as well as the couple's over-all lifestyle. Most important, she wonders, who would get to make the final decision?

THE CLUTTER TRAP

We fall into this trap when we are not systematically undoing old commitments as we take on new ones. As a result, so many promises—new and old—call out for our time and other resources that we may meet none of them or simply fall back on what we were doing before. Many of us have experienced this in our professional lives when we attend management meetings that add new items to our to-do list without removing existing ones. Taken as a whole, the agenda that emerges can be impossible. Let us look at Margaret, a senior executive in a large European firm, who realized she couldn't make new commitments to what she knew had to be done because of existing clutter. She had objectives for more than 50 different key performance indicators at work. Scrambling to achieve those objectives prevented her from taking on new ones. A good rule of thumb for avoiding clutter is to abandon or renegotiate an old com-mitment for every new one you make. Margaret, for example, scheduled an hour a month to cull her diary, canceling meetings as higher priorities arose.

• • •

The final assignment in the course we teach on leading strategic change in organizations invites students to state the commitments they will make (or remake) after the program ends. We are always struck by the diversity of approaches that different students take to this assignment, even after sitting in the same classroom for a semester. This is why we are not offering you hard-and-fast rules for making or remaking your commitments. No such formula is possible for a process that is, by its very nature, highly idiosyncratic and dependent on individual circumstances. But you can manage the gap between what you value and what you do by periodically and systematically reexamining your values and the way you allocate precious resources. Such an exercise can help you take control of your future commitments so that past commitments won't take control of you.

Originally published in January 2005
Reprint R0501H

The Best Advice I Ever Got

DAISY WADEMAN

Executive Summary

A YOUNG MANAGER FACES an impasse in his career. He goes to see his mentor at the company, who closes the office door, offers the young man a chair, recounts a few war stories, and serves up a few specific pointers about the problem at hand. Then, just as the young manager is getting up to leave, the elder executive adds one small kernel of avuncular wisdom—which the junior manager carries with him through the rest of his career.

Such is the nature of business advice. Or is it? The six essays in this article suggest otherwise. Few of the leaders who tell their stories here got their best advice in stereotypical form, as an aphorism or a platitude. For Ogilvy & Mather chief Shelly Lazarus, profound insight came from a remark aimed at relieving the tension of the moment. For Novartis CEO Daniel Vasella, it was an apt comment, made on a snowy day, back when he was a medical resident. For publishing magnate Earl Graves and Starwood Hotels' Barry Sternlicht, advice they received about trust from early bosses took on ever deeper and more practical meaning as their careers progressed. For Goldman Sachs chairman Henry Paulson, Jr., it was as much his father's example as it was a specific piece of advice his father handed down to him. And fashion designer Liz Lange rejects the very notion that there's inherent wisdom in accepting other people's advice.

As these stories demonstrate, people find wisdom when they least expect to, and they never really know what piece of advice will transcend the moment, profoundly affecting how they later make decisions, evaluate people, and examine—and reexamine—their own actions.

A YOUNG MANAGER FACES the first major impasse of his career: His high-profile project is behind schedule and over budget, and his team members are rapidly losing faith in his ability to lead. Disheartened and confused, he goes to see his mentor, a senior executive at the company, looking for direction and encouragement. The mentor shuts his office door and offers the young manager a chair. He recounts a couple of war stories, gives a few specific pointers on how to turn the project around, and then—just as the young manager is getting up to leave—offers up some personal advice. It's just one powerful phrase, a small kernel of avuncular wisdom, but the young manager will carry it with him through the rest of his career. Direct, deliberate, handed down like Grandpa's watch from one generation of managers to the next: Such is the nature of business advice.

Or is it? Three years ago, while still a student at Harvard Business School, I began writing a book, *Remember Who You Are,* a collection of advice to businesspeople from Harvard Business School professors, all told in the form of personal stories. While writing the book, I began to wonder: Where, when, and how do successful executives—as opposed to educators—get their life-changing counsel? The corporation, surely, differs from the classroom. What kind of advice influences senior business leaders as they make their way to the corner office and then as they sit in it?

The following essays suggest some answers to those questions. I interviewed six chief executives from a variety of industries and asked them: What is the best piece of personal advice you've ever gotten that you've used at work? Who gave it to you and in what context? How, specifically, have you used this advice on the job?

The responses I got back—each one edited here into the form of an essay—bore little resemblance to what I had expected. Several interviews began with a sheepish look or a shrug of the shoulders; the majority of executives began by firmly insisting that they had no single anecdote relevant to the questions. Each of them, though, promptly proceeded to dive right in anyway, producing as a group a wide array of tips, strategies, and philosophies for personal success in business. Yet what struck me as much as the messages themselves were the settings and ways in which those messages had been delivered and absorbed.

I had imagined each person receiving a nugget of wisdom while sitting at a valued mentor's knee and immediately recognizing its full import. Instead, much of the advice came by happenstance or in nonbusiness environments and often took decades of professional experience to sink in. Off-the-cuff remarks that the speaker probably wouldn't remember saying have stayed with some of the executives for their entire careers. People these individuals barely know, or advice they just happened to overhear, managed to influence their actions for years. Family relationships or educational settings proved to be as fertile a source of business wisdom as the office. And most surprising of all, few of the leaders I interviewed got their best advice in stereotypical advice form, as an aphorism or a platitude. Instead, it came as a combination of questions, stories, and general attitudes—even, in one case, as a tension-easing joke.

However, each story I heard shared one common, paradoxical characteristic. Gleaned in a particular context—his first day on the job, in the case of former Starwood Hotels CEO Barry Sternlicht, or while engaged in childhood chores, for Goldman Sachs head Henry Paulson—each grain of advice transcended the moment and affected how the executives later made decisions, evaluated people, or examined their own actions. As Ogilvy & Mather's Shelly Lazarus notes, a casual comment can have a sustained effect on day-to-day management and leadership—although, as her first example shows, some wisdom does come in the traditional way.

Shelly Lazarus

Chairman and CEO of the advertising agency Ogilvy & Mather Worldwide

Nine years ago, when I knew I was going to become CEO of this company, I spent three days with its legendary founder, David Ogilvy, at his château in France. It was

March, it was cold and rainy, and we spent the entire time indoors talking about the business. At one point I asked him a question point-blank: David, if you were going to say one thing to me, what would it be? He didn't hesitate in his response. No matter how much time you spend thinking about, worrying about, focusing on, questioning the value of, and evaluating people, it won't be enough, he said. People are the only thing that matters, and the only thing you should think about, because when that part is right, everything else works.

I spend part of every single day hearing David speak that advice, and as a result, I devote a huge amount of time to asking myself: Am I doing enough? Who at Ogilvy do I have to worry about? Who needs another challenge? Who seems a little stale? Who needs a new view on life or a new country to run? David's advice drives not only how I think about and mentor people but also how I form business strategy and make critical decisions.

Let's say, for example, that there was enormous advertising talent in a city where Ogilvy didn't have an office, and the talent refused to leave that city and come to New York, or wherever, to work for us. To me, that's a reason to open a new office. A lot of businesspeople would think primarily about the cost or about whether there were clients in that new city. But ultimately those issues pale in comparison to the need to get, and keep, great talent—great people—at the company.

But let me also offer a more personal piece of advice, if you can call it that. Very early in my career here—I had been at Ogilvy for perhaps two years—I was sitting in my boss's office preparing for an important client meeting. We had to be at the client's at 2 PM, and it was already one o'clock. Suddenly, the media planner on the account arrived in the doorway, looking absolutely panicked. The computer was down, she said, and she couldn't get the numbers out for the media plan we were supposed to be presenting. Now, in those days, when the computer was down, the computer was down; you couldn't just turn it off and reboot. The media planner proceeded to walk into the office and, almost hysterical, began to run in circles, which I've never seen anyone actually do before or since. She had her head in her hands and kept saying, "What am I going to do? What am I going to do?" We watched her going around and around in this sort of frenzy. At a certain point, my boss—a man named Charlie Fredericks—got up, stood in her path, grabbed her by the shoulders, stopped her, and nearly shouted, "What are they going to do to you? Take your children away?"

Not a week goes by that I don't have a Charlie Fredericks moment, one in which I'm forced to stop, apply some real perspective, and then help the people around me do the same. When a business situation seems dire and desperate, people get scared. They freeze like deer in the headlights. They stop being able to deal with the problem or to produce any good work because they're just too frightened. They focus on the crisis itself rather than on what needs to get done.

So, when I have a meeting that's really tense, and when everyone in the office thinks the world is falling apart, I disarm the situation. I'll ask, "Just to be clear, is anyone going to die as a result of our action or inaction? Will Ogilvy go out of business? Will anyone lose a child? Because if that's true, let me know, and I'll get significantly more agitated." It just makes everyone laugh, and when we're done laughing, I tell them, "Now let's really focus and get this problem sorted out."

This technique can be used anytime people get wrapped up in the sense of crisis, but it's particularly useful when people get *really* emotional. And in advertising, that happens when a long-term client puts the agency under review or decides to go with another firm, because at that moment there's little to gain but an enormous amount to lose.

In 1991, we got fired by American Express. They took away the big, sexy stuff—the brand work, most of the television—and gave it to another agency, leaving us with the little co-op stuff, the joint promotions with service establishments. American Express had been with us since the early sixties, and at one point they were our largest client. But, as David Ogilvy noted when he phoned me at home that Saturday to tell me, the truth is that clients come and go: You'll always win another one, and another will go away.

The real problem came when people within the company became dispirited and demotivated, engulfed by crisis, felt differently about the work they were doing, and were ready to walk away in a huff, wanting nothing more to do with it. The challenge, therefore, for me was not simply to win back a big account. It was to motivate the people within Ogilvy to forget about the catastrophe and focus on the work. Gathering everyone together, I told them, "What's happened has happened. And if you're not interested in hanging in there, then go away. Just go away. But if you're ready to believe again and sit around this table and go at the problem with all the heart we have, with all our understanding of the brand, and with all our belief, then let's get to work and see if we can win back the hearts and minds of the people at American Express." It took 11 months, but we won that account back.

David Ogilvy's advice and Charlie Fredericks' comment, while very different in tone and message, go to the same fundamental issue. Advertising is an ideas business: That's all we are. And ideas don't come from the air; they come from human beings. If our firm doesn't have people who can generate great ideas and keep their perspective and good judgment intact even in tough circumstances, so they can develop those ideas in compelling ways for our clients, then we don't have anything.

Daniel Vasella, M.D.

Chairman and CEO of the pharmaceutical company Novartis

There are many ways to learn. We learn from theory, observation, and our own practical experience. Invariably, emotions deepen learning, especially when a comment or an experience hurts or pleases, offering new insights and generating new ways of coping with a challenge. Lessons that fit one's character may be easier to assimilate, but in the end the ones that surprise us, that don't fit our usual patterns, are more likely to be remembered.

Of course I learned from every supervisor I had—through positive and negative examples. I can't, however, really say that I learned this or learned that directly from the advice of a boss. Good advice, I think, often emerges from discussions, particularly ones that are more reflective or relaxed than normal. During these kinds of conversations, learning occurs in an osmotic way. In fact, later on you find it difficult to recall the exact context or details of the conversation itself, but from it you absorb a piece of wisdom that stays with you over time. I've had several experiences like this at very different periods in my life. Let me share two examples.

The first incident occurred during my medical residency. Every morning at our hospital began with a short meeting, what we called the morning report. We physicians coming on duty were briefed about what had happened with our patients overnight, and we heard about the new patients. We figured out what needed to be done that day and who should be responsible for what. The meeting was conducted in a highly disciplined manner; my boss disliked it profoundly when people came in late. In fact, being tardy was unacceptable.

One winter morning, however, the weather was horrible, and the roads were covered with ice and snow. As I drove to work, I realized I hadn't left enough time. Arriving at the meeting 15, maybe 20, minutes late, I was embarrassed and began apologizing as I sat down in the conference room. But my boss interrupted me. "On a day like today," he responded, "only stupid people are on time."

That one remark had a deep impact on me. It made me realize that sometimes the generally accepted, traditional rule is the worst possible one to follow. When you're setting priorities in any situation, you have to look at their relative importance and at the circumstances. And you have to be willing to change your own rules.

The second incident came just a few months ago, when I was in Singapore. I met with Senior Minister Lee Kuan Yew, the country's first and longtime prime minister, who has been criticized in the West for his authoritarian rule even as he created Southeast Asia's most successful state. We spoke for about an hour. He told me about the Vietnam War, about America's ultimate decision to pull out of the region, and about how that situation related, and didn't relate, to Indonesia's and Singapore's current challenges with religious fundamentalism. As we were finishing our conversation, he said, "You know, it is crunch time now." Clearly, he would not hesitate to confront an opponent. He accepted that both sides might get hurt in the process but was willing to exercise the power that would lead to victory—however negative other people's reactions might be.

In the first example, my boss was offering an opinion and, in the second, Lee Kuan Yew was telling me about himself, his thinking, his determination, and his country. But in both cases, the insight I gained came not in the moment itself or from what was said but from stepping back, from thinking about what had happened, from pondering what I had been told and how I had reacted emotionally. And both situations continue to affect me practically—to influence how I act at work, how I evaluate options and alternatives, and how I analyze myself and my actions.

My experience being late that morning at the hospital years ago has given me a lifelong tolerance for mistakes—my own and others—as what may appear at first to be a mistake might sometimes be the only right way forward. It also has made me empathetic toward employees when, for example, they are conscientious and make an effort but, for whatever reason, don't manage to get a task or project done. It has taught me to reconsider the appropriateness of my own rules from time to time and to review them in the light of changing circumstances.

The "crunch time" comment, though it came recently in my life, will stick with me, creating a new way of looking at and thinking about difficult situations and how I want to approach them. Where do I tend to avoid crunches—and why? How can I determine when I'm going into a crunch, and how can I willingly and consciously decide to do what's right and necessary, despite scrutiny and criticism?

Already, I've begun looking back on certain events as crunches. I've thought a lot about crunches in relation to the way we went about bidding for Aventis, for example. We were warned by the French government not to begin merger talks because the government preferred that Aventis merge with Sanofi-Synthelabo instead. So the question was: Should we simply give in or do our job despite the possibility of a confrontation? Now I see that as a crunch time: We had to forget about the reaction of the government and the press. In the end we did walk away, but we did it for business reasons, not to avoid a crunch.

On reflection, perhaps these two particular comments continue to resonate with me because of my professional background and training. As a physician, you are keenly aware of the limits of your knowledge and expertise. You can never master every situation or specialty; you constantly have to seek help from experts in other fields. You admit your lack of knowledge to anybody you think can help you cure the patient. But when you've gotten the facts and know what's wrong with the person, you must be confident enough to go ahead and order the treatment—even if others doubt you or express divergent views—because decisive and rapid action can mean life or death for the patient. In business, the stakes may not be life or death, but clear, disciplined thinking and prompt action are also usually vital to success.

Liz Lange

Founder and president/designer of the fashion company Liz Lange Maternity

Three years ago, I had a successful company that designed and sold fashionable, upscale clothing for pregnant women. We had stand-alone stores on Madison Avenue and in Beverly Hills, and an exclusive licensing deal with Nike. We were in conversations with a major upscale department-store chain about opening boutiques in each of their locations around the country.

At the same time, I began talking to someone else—Target—about a line of maternity wear for their stores that would be chic but available at a much lower price point. Not surprisingly, nearly everyone I spoke to thought that designing Liz Lange–branded clothes for a huge discount retailer was an absolutely terrible idea, that partnering with Target would kill the brand. The high end just cannot coexist with the low end, they said, because the customer doesn't want to pay $200 for a sweater at one store that she can buy for $25 at another. The CEO of the department-store company told me that if I went with Target, any deal with them was off. But instead of getting bogged down and listening to the naysayers, I did what I think is one of the most important things for a businessperson, particularly an entrepreneur, to do: I ignored all the outside advice and listened to my instincts.

Now, no one ever told me, "Liz, ignore outside advice"—or least, not in those very words. My husband, however, is also an entrepreneur—he's designed mathematical models for trading derivatives, which he licenses to places like Goldman Sachs—and we talk a lot about the entrepreneurial experience. He's very supportive of what I do and is very inspirational to me. He likes to tell the story about the founders of Xerox, who initially had difficulty getting funding. Venture capitalists would look at the prototype of a Xerox machine and ask, "But who would want to make a copy?" His point is that to start a company, particularly in a brand-new area, you've got to block out the noise around you and just forge ahead.

To me, the idea of offering stylish maternity clothes at an affordable price point made sense. I had gotten e-mails from about a zillion customers saying they wished I also had a more affordable line. (I should add that people also told me that I shouldn't be reading customer e-mail, that as the head of a growing company, I had more important things to do.) Some of the e-mails I got were polite ("I want to dress that way when I'm pregnant but can't afford it"), and some were pretty nasty ("How dare you charge $150 for a pair of pants?"). Instinctively, I knew my customers would understand that what they were getting in the boutiques was different from what they were getting at Target, and I imagined even really well-heeled customers buying little $15 "Liz Lange for Target" T-shirts, then buying expensive jackets at the store on Madison Avenue and mixing them up, and that would be cool.

The proposed deal with Target made excellent sense for my company, as well. If we had linked up with the fancy department-store chain, we'd have been producing the clothes for maybe 30 in-store shops and would have to take back merchandise that didn't sell. As it turned out, Target would produce and own the goods they carried, offer them in 1,200 stores, and launch a major ad campaign—with the proceeds of all this made payable to the order of Liz Lange.

So, despite the criticism, I got on a plane and flew to Minneapolis. I met with about 15 people at Target and just talked about who I am and what our company does. I thought, this is a good idea for them and a good idea for me and a good idea for the customers, too, and it will logically happen because it makes sense. A week or two later, Target called back, and we struck a deal.

Maybe this makes me sound like Mr. Magoo, just blindly going through life, which isn't the case at all. I'm very competitive, I'm up at night worrying about the company, and I put a lot of pressure on myself to stay ahead of other maternity-wear designers. But at every phase in the growth of this business, I've had to block out the noise, not think about the negative.

When I started my company seven years ago, stylish high-end maternity wear was an oxymoron. Maternity clothing was mostly prints and smocks, and way too cutesy—as if the woman was morphing into a baby herself, rather than having one. All the pregnant women I knew, who worked on Wall Street or at magazines or wherever, were always complaining, "I've got a board meeting today, an office party Thursday, and I'm going to the Hamptons this weekend, and I don't have a thing to wear."

So I began taking a sort of informal poll, asking people, "If I could design a really great pair of pants in a terrific stretch fabric that would cost $175, would you buy it?" Most said no. Later, I started approaching major retailers, explaining my idea. Each one of them said the same thing: Maternity is a terrible business because a woman is only pregnant for nine months, and she won't shop for beautiful, expensive clothes for that short a time in her life. One even told me to save the money I was going to invest in the business and treat myself to a nice shopping trip to Paris. Instead, I opened a tiny office on East 61st Street in Manhattan, found a factory to make up some samples, and began calling the women I knew who were pregnant. Don't get me wrong. Many days during that first year—days when no one called and I had no appointments—I spent literally curled up in my bedroom worrying that the naysayers were right: This *is* a terrible idea. It's never going to work. What am I *doing?*

But pretty soon my phone was ringing off the hook, and the women who said they wouldn't spend $175 on pants were clamoring for the product. When Nike approached me a few years later about cobranding a line of maternity active apparel, even my own lawyers told me I was wasting money paying their fees because the deal would never happen: Nike only cobranded with athletes, never with designers, and particularly not with a tiny firm like mine. When I started thinking about designing very fitted maternity clothes, my customers resisted the idea of wearing them. Now, the Liz Lange for Nike line is thriving, and at our boutiques the tube top and stretch leather pants are best-selling products.

As an entrepreneur, I speak to groups all the time, to people who have started companies themselves or who are thinking about it. Every time I speak, I say how important it is to ignore, or at least carefully filter, outside advice. And every time, a hundred people will line up after the speech, and each one will say the same thing to me: "My God, yes, this is exactly what happened to me. You've just put it into words." Regardless of what field they're in or what kind of firm they've started, they've all been told "no." The experience is universal. Customers and investors will never have your vision for the product because they can't touch it and feel it in advance. It's your job to follow your instincts, prop yourself up, and trust that if you build it, they will come.

Henry M. Paulson, Jr.

Chairman and CEO of the financial services firm Goldman Sachs

Over the course of my childhood and adolescence, I received powerful guidance from my father, who gave the same piece of advice many times and in many different forms. It wasn't about one specific action or situation but, instead, about a habit and a general philosophy, about a way of looking at work. Real happiness, he said, comes from striving to do something that isn't easy— and then succeeding in doing it.

My dad was a businessman, though not a particularly successful one. He worked in a business that his father had started and then opened his own management consultancy that provided sales-training material. At the same time, he was very much a farmer at heart. He had a ranch in Stuart, Florida, in the days before that area was developed, and when he needed to move back home to run the family business, we lived on a small farm in Illinois.

From the time I was really young—five or six years old—he had me out pushing wheelbarrows filled with building bricks or mowing the lawn or doing daily chores on the farm, mucking out the horse stalls, baling and stacking hay. When I woke up in the morning, he would hand me a list of the things I needed to do (my brother says he still has dreams about these lists). When I'd finished my work, he would come out to inspect. We had a seven- or eight-acre lawn and, in the fall, raking up all the leaves just seemed like an interminable task. When I was done, my father would walk around, and if he found leaves that hadn't been pulled out of the bushes, he'd tell me, "You left a holiday here." When all the leaves were gone, he'd praise me for a job well done.

In many ways, my father glorified work. But he was definitely not an all-work-and-no-play kind of guy. He didn't think that working hard was in and of itself a virtue, and he didn't think that you should suffer while you were working, either. Dad believed in taking vacations and loved to take us skiing, fishing, and on canoe trips up in Canada. We kept horses and, when we were finished with our day's chores, he'd saddle up the horses and take us riding and teach us bird calls—meadowlark, bobolink, scarlet tanager. Or on a hot summer day, he'd tell us to go over to the town pool—but only when our work was done.

His point was that if you set yourself a large, difficult goal, you could get great pleasure from striving to reach it, tremendous confidence from actually reaching it, and satisfaction from completing it. *Then* you could celebrate your success and go do something fun.

My dad's influence has stayed with me throughout my adult life and my career at Goldman Sachs. His advice has affected me in small ways: To this day, for example, I tend to work quickly. I'd rather be out getting things done, doing the least attractive tasks first so that I will have more time to spend with my family. But the advice has affected me in larger ways as well.

In my early days at the firm, I was assigned to cover clients that Goldman had never done business with before—Caterpillar, Sara Lee, Kellogg, Santa Fe

Railway—and, as a young calling officer, I had to work to build up relationships with them. Like working eight acres of unraked leaves, it was a daunting task. I had to come up with ideas, make endless trips to see the clients, and work to build their trust so that they turned to us rather than their traditional banks when they needed to execute an important transaction.

When raking leaves, you can see definite progress. You can say, "I've got two acres done, now three, now four." But building relationships was more difficult and frustrating than raking leaves in that it was a multiyear, as opposed to a multiday, process. Many times when I was certain that I'd made headway with the clients (and probably had done so), they would still turn to a traditional bank to complete a transaction. It was like having a wind come up and watching the leaves I'd already raked blown back onto the lawn (a not uncommon experience). Nonetheless, I usually found that if I didn't take shortcuts and I applied myself diligently to the matter at hand—whether it was a lawn covered with leaves or a competitor's client—my efforts would be rewarded.

Even as a young banker, though, I scheduled regular vacations. The wilderness canoeing and camping trips our family took reflected my dad's influence, too. Sometimes I'd be paddling a canoe into a stiff headwind in the rain, and I'd have my daughter or son in the bow, and I'd think, "Why am I doing this?" Most people wouldn't consider this leisure. We worked hard: carrying canoes and swatting mosquitoes and going over these tough portages to get to a beautiful, isolated lake. But once we were there, that lake was our lake. We could take great pride in getting there, and it was just us and the loons and the beavers, clear water for swimming, blueberry pancakes for breakfast, and fresh lake trout for dinner.

Earl G. Graves

Founder, chairman, and CEO of Earl G. Graves, Limited, whose businesses include Black Enterprise *magazine*

In the mid-1960s, I went to work as a salesman for a real estate developer by the name of Valerio Cardinale. Cardinale was prosperous, successful at what he did, and a man of enormous integrity. He was a very serious fellow; one of his sons, also in the real estate business, had been killed in a car accident, and you got the sense that the tragedy weighed on him constantly.

Early on, Cardinale gave me two pieces of advice. "Mr. Graves," he told me (the man was 20 years my senior and very formal), "the first thing you need to know here is that we treat everyone the same, whether it's a multimillionaire real estate developer or one of our tenants. Just to be clear, I'm not going to spend a full hour with someone who's come to the office to complain about his rent, but I'll be as generous with my time as I reasonably can."

His second piece of advice was, "Trust people." Now what did he mean by that? Well, at the simplest level, he was talking about the practical need for trust. Working for Cardinale, I had quickly realized that I was very good at selling, but I constantly found myself doubting people—the mortgage bankers, the other real estate developers, and so on. There was a good basis for my skepticism, Cardinale confirmed, but if I couldn't put my trust in other people, I was never going to get anything done.

But his advice goes beyond that. Trust also enables you to leverage yourself, to delegate responsibility to people who can make you more effective or carry out your ideas. For example, when I ask my assistant to place an important call, I assume that it will get done—and quickly. This trust in others is now implicit in all of my interactions; I don't run around doubting the people who work with me.

Let me offer a very recent example. When we were preparing our October 2004 issue, the president and CEO of *Black Enterprise*—who happens to be my son, Butch—came to me and said he wanted to put Barack Obama on the cover. We had a great article about Obama for the issue, on his life and political career and his run for the Senate. Now, Obama had not yet given the address at the Democratic Convention when we were making this decision, and the election itself was still some ways off. So I asked Butch what the other choice was—you always have two choices for what goes on the cover—and it was a feature story on the "50 Best Colleges for African-Americans." This was a great piece that a lot of our readership would be focused on. But when Butch comes to me and says, "This is a worthwhile article," I take him seriously, and Barack ended up on the front of the book—ultimately the right choice for us.

Trust brings out the best in people: If they sense they are trusted, they will rise to the occasion. Let me illustrate that with a story about someone trusting me. I volunteered for Robert Kennedy, back when he was a senator. One of my early tasks was to put together an event—a Christmas party—for him. Previous events prepared by volunteers had been disasters, and I worked hard to be sure that this one was well organized. During the party, Kennedy leaned over to me and asked, "What's your name again?" "Graves," I answered. Soon after, I went to work for Kennedy full-time as an aide. The fact that the party came off without a hitch apparently impressed him: He could count on me to do what I said I would.

Kennedy, like me, could be skeptical of people and their motivations. Often, when heading into a meeting or political rally, he would turn to his staff and say, "Better zipper up your pockets before going in there!" But he had absolute trust in the folks working for him, and we responded to that trust by doing everything we could to live up to his expectations. He could have said to his staff, "I'd like to play basketball in this office tomorrow," and we would have set to work that evening raising the ceiling, putting in a hardwood floor, and setting up the nets. That's the kind of dedication, engendered by trust, every manager dreams of.

Barry S. Sternlicht

Former chairman and chief executive officer of Starwood Hotels & Resorts Worldwide and currently its executive chairman and chief design officer

I've been very inspired by certain words of advice people have given me over the years, things that suddenly struck me as terribly important at the time, and I think about them often. It's as if they're branded on my brain. They're life defining.

As a result, I'm just a treasure trove of sayings. "Pretty good is not good enough": I heard Mel Karmazin, who was the president of Viacom and who had run CBS, say that in a speech recently, and it resonated with me. When you're running a company, you get a lot of that. "How're things going?" I'll ask someone. "Pretty good," they'll say. (How about excellent? Who strives for "pretty good"?)

I've got others, too. "Hope is not a business strategy." "Luck is where preparation meets opportunity." "Perseverance is genius in disguise"—that one actually came from a fortune cookie, but I think it's very true. I've never considered myself brilliant, but throughout my career, I've put my shoulder to the wheel and worked hard, and thankfully it's paid off.

One of the most important pieces of advice I've gotten, however, is slightly more complex; it doesn't boil down so neatly into a fortune-cookie saying, but I think about it constantly.

When I graduated from Harvard Business School in 1986, I ended up at a firm called JMB Realty in Chicago. I had no real estate experience, but I wanted to learn how to do deals. My first day on the job, my boss sat me down in his office and said, "Let me tell you the rules of engagement. The first thing you have to do is always tell the truth. I want to know the truth about everything—all the facts—that concerns what we're investing in. And then I want your opinion on those facts. But I want to make sure you understand the difference between the two. If you can do all that, I'll know you have good judgment, and if you have good judgment, then you can go anywhere in this world and anywhere in this company. Without good judgment, you'll never succeed in business."

That advice is the cornerstone of how I've approached doing deals throughout my career and everything I've done as CEO. In order to build an organization, you have to be able to delegate, and in order to delegate, you have to have confidence in the people working for you. You have to know that they're thorough in their research, that they gather all the facts they need, that they tell the truth about what they've found, that they form sensible opinions based on the data they've collected, and that they grasp the difference between fact and speculation.

Sounds pretty easy, right? Wrong. As I myself discovered soon after getting that advice, even gathering all the relevant data on a certain project can be harder than you think. For one of my first deals at JMB, I was asked to acquire an apartment building in California, and I decided I was going to impress everyone with my brilliance. I spent days and days at this property. I talked to all the tenants. I measured the distance between the blades of grass on the lawn. I knew everything about this asset. But when I sat down with the head of our company's investment committee, he asked, "How far apart are the parking lot stripes?" I said, "What? I know what the rents are. I know Mrs. Smith has a kid in college and is moving out next week, and we can re-rent her apartment. Why do you need to know that?" And he answered, "Because you can re-stripe the spaces and make more of them. Large cars take 16 feet, and small cars only need 13. And those spaces are worth $50,000 each because of the income on them." At that point I thought, "Oh my God, the things I don't know I don't know." I hadn't even known to ask the question. Sure, I had told the truth and offered an opinion, but I didn't have all the facts I needed to form it.

Even with all the facts in front of them, however—even after an extraordinarily rigorous due diligence that takes into account those parking lot stripes—some brilliant people still can't form good opinions because they can't figure out what that data in front of them means. Others are willing to look at the facts and ignore what's there, to be a little less than truthful.

Just out of college, I worked as a consultant in New York City, and I remember once being asked to put together a chart plotting two variables against each other on *x* and *y* axes. The resulting scatter chart had points all over the page. The partner at the time came in, covered the dots on one side of the chart and then the dots on the other, leaving a straight upward slope, and said "Look—there's a perfect correlation." And I said, "You can't do that!" Your opinion has to be based on the data and not the other way around; you can't just retrofit the facts to what you want to be the truth.

Even worse, however, is when people offer opinions drawn from no hard data at all, when their viewpoint is based on what they simply hope is true. Often when we lose a contract to another company, our person in charge of the deal will tell me, "Well, they underbid us." And I'll reply, "Do you know that for certain? Or is it just your opinion?" I want to know if it's a hard fact that we were underbid or if he's just hoping that's the case or if he's protecting his behind because he lost the deal.

When we bought Westin Hotels, the CFO of another hotel company said it had been a lousy transaction and that we overpaid. At the time, he was very famous, and I was nobody. But he didn't know the deal, he didn't know how I'd structured the deal, he didn't know the price I'd paid, and he didn't know the assets that were included. Business decisions need to be made on real data—on an unflinching assessment and analysis of how your company is doing. When you start making decisions based on what you wish were true, you're going to make some pretty bad calls.

I repeat this advice from my first boss to people early in their careers, and I like to tell this story to all of our new employees. But it's especially important as you become more senior. When you get higher up on the ladder, and particularly as CEO, you get this intellectual illusion of invulnerability. And that's when you can lose your good judgment. You lose your fear because you're successful, and you think you've got it all figured out. But if you can resist that and follow my JMB boss's advice—by sticking to the facts, being honest, developing solid opinions, and otherwise demonstrating good judgment—it will keep you out of trouble.

Originally published in January 2005
Reprint R0501C

Managing Your Boss

JOHN J. GABARRO AND JOHN P. KOTTER

Executive Summary

IN THIS CLASSIC HBR ARTICLE, first published in 1980, Gabarro and Kotter advise readers to devote time and energy to managing their relationships with their bosses. The authors aren't talking about showering supervisors with flattery; rather, they ask readers to understand that the manager-boss relationship is one of mutual dependence. Bosses need cooperation, reliability, and honesty from their direct reports. Managers, for their part, rely on bosses for making connections with the rest of the company, for setting priorities, and for obtaining critical resources. It only makes sense to work at making the relationship operate as smoothly as possible.

   Successfully managing your relationship with your boss requires that you have a good understanding of your supervisor and of yourself, particularly strengths, weaknesses, work styles, and needs. Once you are aware of what impedes or facilitates communication with your boss, you can take actions to improve your relationship. You can usually establish a way of working together that fits both of you, that is characterized by unambiguous mutual expectations, and that makes both of you more productive and effective.

No doubt, some managers will resent that on top of all their other duties, they must also take responsibility for their relationships with their bosses. But these managers fail to realize that by doing so, they can actually simplify their jobs, eliminating potentially severe problems and improving productivity.

A QUARTER-CENTURY AGO, John Gabarro and John Kotter introduced a powerful new lens through which to view the manager–boss relationship: one that recognized the mutual dependence of the participants.

The fact is, bosses need cooperation, reliability, and honesty from their direct reports. Managers, for their part, rely on bosses for making connections with the rest of the company, for setting priorities, and for obtaining critical resources. If the relationship between you and your boss is rocky, then it is you who must begin to manage it. When you take the time to cultivate a productive working relationship—by understanding your boss's strengths and weaknesses, priorities, and work style—everyone wins.

In the 25 years since it was published, this article has truly improved the practice of management. Its simple yet powerful advice has changed the way people work, enhanced countless manager–boss relationships, and improved the performance of corporations in ways that show up on the bottom line. Over the years, it has become a staple at business schools and corporate training programs worldwide.

To many people, the phrase "managing your boss" may sound unusual or suspicious. Because of the traditional top-down emphasis in most organizations, it is not obvious why you need to manage relationships upward—unless, of course, you would do so for personal or political reasons. But we are not referring to political maneuvering or to apple polishing. We are using the term to mean the process of consciously working with your superior to obtain the best possible results for you, your boss, and the company.

Recent studies suggest that effective managers take time and effort to manage not only relationships with their subordinates but also those with their bosses. These studies also show that this essential aspect of management is sometimes ignored by otherwise talented and aggressive managers. Indeed, some managers who actively and effectively supervise subordinates, products, markets, and technologies assume an almost passively reactive stance vis-à-vis their bosses. Such a stance almost always hurts them and their companies.

If you doubt the importance of managing your relationship with your boss or how difficult it is to do so effectively, consider for a moment the following sad but telling story:

Frank Gibbons was an acknowledged manufacturing genius in his industry and, by any profitability standard, a very effective executive. In 1973, his strengths propelled him into the position of vice president of manufacturing for the second largest and most profitable company in its industry. Gibbons was not, however, a good manager of people. He knew this, as did others in his company and his industry. Recognizing this weakness, the president made sure that those who reported to Gibbons were good at working with people and could compensate for his limitations. The arrangement worked well.

In 1975, Philip Bonnevie was promoted into a position reporting to Gibbons. In keeping with the previous pattern, the president selected Bonnevie because he had an excellent track record and a reputation for being good with people. In making that selection, however, the president neglected to notice that, in his rapid rise through the organization, Bonnevie had always had good-to-excellent bosses. He had never been forced to manage a relationship with a difficult boss. In retrospect, Bonnevie admits he had never thought that managing his boss was a part of his job.

Fourteen months after he started working for Gibbons, Bonnevie was fired. During that same quarter, the company reported a net loss for the first time in seven years. Many of those who were close to these events say that they don't really understand what happened. This much is known, however: While the company was bringing out a major new product—a process that required sales, engineering, and manufacturing groups to coordinate decisions very carefully—a whole series of misunderstandings and bad feelings developed between Gibbons and Bonnevie.

For example, Bonnevie claims Gibbons was aware of and had accepted Bonnevie's decision to use a new type of machinery to make the new product; Gibbons swears he did not. Furthermore, Gibbons claims he made it clear to Bonnevie that the introduction of the product was too important to the company in the short run to take any major risks.

As a result of such misunderstandings, planning went awry: A new manufacturing plant was built that could not produce the new product designed by engineering, in the volume desired by sales, at a cost agreed on by the executive committee. Gibbons blamed Bonnevie for the mistake. Bonnevie blamed Gibbons.

Of course, one could argue that the problem here was caused by Gibbons's inability to manage his subordinates. But one can make just as strong a case that the problem was related to Bonnevie's inability to manage his boss. Remember, Gibbons was not having difficulty with any other subordinates. Moreover, given the personal price paid by Bonnevie (being fired and having his reputation within the industry severely tarnished), there was little consolation in saying the problem was that Gibbons was poor at managing subordinates. Everyone already knew that.

We believe that the situation could have turned out differently had Bonnevie been more adept at understanding Gibbons and at managing his relationship with him. In this case, an inability to manage upward was unusually costly. The company lost $2 million to $5 million, and Bonnevie's career was, at least temporarily, disrupted. Many less costly cases similar to this probably occur regularly in all major corporations, and the cumulative effect can be very destructive.

Misreading the Boss–Subordinate Relationship

People often dismiss stories like the one we just related as being merely cases of personality conflict. Because two people can on occasion be psychologically or temperamentally incapable of working together, this can be an apt description. But more often, we have found, a personality conflict is only a part of the problem— sometimes a very small part.

Bonnevie did not just have a different personality from Gibbons, he also made or had unrealistic assumptions and expectations about the very nature of boss–subordinate relationships. Specifically, he did not recognize that his relationship to Gibbons involved *mutual dependence* between two *fallible* human beings. Failing to recognize this, a manager typically either avoids trying to manage his or her relationship with a boss or manages it ineffectively.

Some people behave as if their bosses were not very dependent on them. They fail to see how much the boss needs their help and cooperation to do his or her job effectively. These people refuse to acknowledge that the boss can be severely hurt by their actions and needs cooperation, dependability, and honesty from them.

Some people see themselves as not very dependent on their bosses. They gloss over how much help and information they need from the boss in order to perform their own jobs well. This superficial view is particularly damaging when a manager's job and decisions affect other parts of the organization, as was the case in Bonnevie's situation. A manager's immediate boss can play a critical role in linking the manager to the rest of the organization, making sure the manager's priorities are consistent with organizational needs, and in securing the resources the manager needs to perform well. Yet some managers need to see themselves as practically self-sufficient, as not needing the critical information and resources a boss can supply.

Many managers, like Bonnevie, assume that the boss will magically know what information or help their subordinates need and provide it to them. Certainly, some

bosses do an excellent job of caring for their subordinates in this way, but for a manager to expect that from
all bosses is dangerously unrealistic. A more reasonable
expectation for managers to have is that modest help
will be forthcoming. After all, bosses are only human.
Most really effective managers accept this fact and
assume primary responsibility for their own careers and
development. They make a point of seeking the information and help they need to do a job instead of waiting for
their bosses to provide it.

In light of the foregoing, it seems to us that managing
a situation of mutual dependence among fallible human
beings requires the following:

1. You have a good understanding of the other person
and yourself, especially regarding strengths, weaknesses,
work styles, and needs.

2. You use this information to develop and manage a
healthy working relationship—one that is compatible
with both people's work styles and assets, is characterized by mutual expectations, and meets the most critical
needs of the other person.

This combination is essentially what we have found
highly effective managers doing.

Understanding the Boss

Managing your boss requires that you gain an understanding of the boss and his or her context, as well as
your own situation. All managers do this to some degree,
but many are not thorough enough.

At a minimum, you need to appreciate your boss's
goals and pressures, his or her strengths and weaknesses.
What are your boss's organizational and personal objectives, and what are his or her pressures, especially those
from his or her own boss and others at the same level?

What are your boss's long suits and blind spots? What is the preferred style of working? Does your boss like to get information through memos, formal meetings, or phone calls? Does he or she thrive on conflict or try to minimize it? Without this information, a manager is flying blind when dealing with the boss, and unnecessary conflicts, misunderstandings, and problems are inevitable.

In one situation we studied, a top-notch marketing manager with a superior performance record was hired into a company as a vice president "to straighten out the marketing and sales problems." The company, which was having financial difficulties, had recently been acquired by a larger corporation. The president was eager to turn it around and gave the new marketing vice president free rein—at least initially. Based on his previous experience, the new vice president correctly diagnosed that greater market share was needed for the company and that strong product management was required to bring that about. Following that logic, he made a number of pricing decisions aimed at increasing high-volume business.

When margins declined and the financial situation did not improve, however, the president increased pressure on the new vice president. Believing that the situation would eventually correct itself as the company gained back market share, the vice president resisted the pressure.

When by the second quarter, margins and profits had still failed to improve, the president took direct control over all pricing decisions and put all items on a set level of margin, regardless of volume. The new vice president began to find himself shut out by the president, and their relationship deteriorated. In fact, the vice president found the president's behavior bizarre. Unfortunately, the president's new pricing scheme also failed to increase margins, and by the fourth quarter, both the president and the vice president were fired.

What the new vice president had not known until it was too late was that improving marketing and sales had been only *one* of the president's goals. His most immediate goal had been to make the company more profitable—quickly.

Nor had the new vice president known that his boss was invested in this short-term priority for personal as well as business reasons. The president had been a strong advocate of the acquisition within the parent company, and his personal credibility was at stake.

The vice president made three basic errors. He took information supplied to him at face value, he made assumptions in areas where he had no information, and—what was most damaging—he never actively tried to clarify what his boss's objectives were. As a result, he ended up taking actions that were actually at odds with the president's priorities and objectives.

Managers who work effectively with their bosses do not behave this way. They seek out information about the boss's goals and problems and pressures. They are alert for opportunities to question the boss and others around him or her to test their assumptions. They pay attention to clues in the boss's behavior. Although it is imperative that they do this especially when they begin working with a new boss, effective managers also do this on an ongoing basis because they recognize that priorities and concerns change.

Being sensitive to a boss's work style can be crucial, especially when the boss is new. For example, a new president who was organized and formal in his approach replaced a man who was informal and intuitive. The new president worked best when he had written reports. He also preferred formal meetings with set agendas.

One of his division managers realized this need and worked with the new president to identify the kinds and frequency of information and reports that the president wanted. This manager also made a point of sending background information and brief agendas ahead of time for their discussions. He found that with this type of preparation their meetings were very useful. Another interesting result was, he found that with adequate preparation his new boss was even more effective at brainstorming problems than his more informal and intuitive predecessor had been.

In contrast, another division manager never fully understood how the new boss's work style differed from that of his predecessor. To the degree that he did sense it, he experienced it as too much control. As a result, he seldom sent the new president the background information he needed, and the president never felt fully prepared for meetings with the manager. In fact, the president spent much of the time when they met trying to get information that he felt he should have had earlier. The boss experienced these meetings as frustrating and inefficient, and the subordinate often found himself thrown off guard by the questions that the president asked. Ultimately, this division manager resigned.

The difference between the two division managers just described was not so much one of ability or even adaptability. Rather, one of the men was more sensitive to his boss's work style and to the implications of his boss's needs than the other was.

Understanding Yourself

The boss is only one-half of the relationship. You are the other half, as well as the part over which you have more

direct control. Developing an effective working relationship requires, then, that you know your own needs,
strengths and weaknesses, and personal style.

You are not going to change either your basic personality structure or that of your boss. But you can become
aware of what it is about you that impedes or facilitates
working with your boss and, with that awareness, take
actions that make the relationship more effective.

For example, in one case we observed, a manager
and his superior ran into problems whenever they dis-
agreed. The boss's typical response was to harden his
position and overstate it. The manager's reaction was
then to raise the ante and intensify the forcefulness of
his argument. In doing this, he channeled his anger into
sharpening his attacks on the logical fallacies he saw in
his boss's assumptions. His boss in turn would become
even more adamant about holding his original position.
Predictably, this escalating cycle resulted in the subordinate avoiding whenever possible any topic of potential conflict with his boss.

In discussing this problem with his peers, the manager discovered that his reaction to the boss was typical
of how he generally reacted to counterarguments—
but with a difference. His response would overwhelm
his peers but not his boss. Because his attempts to discuss this problem with his boss were unsuccessful, he
concluded that the only way to change the situation
was to deal with his own instinctive reactions. Whenever the two reached an impasse, he would check his
own impatience and suggest that they break up and
think about it before getting together again. Usually
when they renewed their discussion, they had digested
their differences and were more able to work them
through.

Gaining this level of self-awareness and acting on it are difficult but not impossible. For example, by reflecting over his past experiences, a young manager learned that he was not very good at dealing with difficult and emotional issues where people were involved. Because he disliked those issues and realized that his instinctive responses to them were seldom very good, he developed a habit of touching base with his boss whenever such a problem arose. Their discussions always surfaced ideas and approaches the manager had not considered. In many cases, they also identified specific actions the boss could take to help.

Although a superior–subordinate relationship is one of mutual dependence, it is also one in which the subordinate is typically more dependent on the boss than the other way around. This dependence inevitably results in the subordinate feeling a certain degree of frustration, sometimes anger, when his actions or options are constrained by his boss's decisions. This is a normal part of life and occurs in the best of relationships. The way in which a manager handles these frustrations largely depends on his or her predisposition toward dependence on authority figures.

Some people's instinctive reaction under these circumstances is to resent the boss's authority and to rebel against the boss's decisions. Sometimes a person will escalate a conflict beyond what is appropriate. Seeing the boss almost as an institutional enemy, this type of manager will often, without being conscious of it, fight with the boss just for the sake of fighting. The subordinate's reactions to being constrained are usually strong and sometimes impulsive. He or she sees the boss as someone who, by virtue of the role, is a hindrance to progress, an obstacle to be circumvented or at best tolerated.

Psychologists call this pattern of reactions counterdependent behavior. Although a counterdependent person
is difficult for most superiors to manage and usually has
a history of strained relationships with superiors, this
sort of manager is apt to have even more trouble with a
boss who tends to be directive or authoritarian. When
the manager acts on his or her negative feelings, often in
subtle and nonverbal ways, the boss sometimes does
become the enemy. Sensing the subordinate's latent hos-
tility, the boss will lose trust in the subordinate or his or
her judgment and then behave even less openly.

Paradoxically, a manager with this type of predisposition is often a good manager of his or her own people.
He or she will many times go out of the way to get support for them and will not hesitate to go to bat for
them.

At the other extreme are managers who swallow their
anger and behave in a very compliant fashion when the
boss makes what they know to be a poor decision. These
managers will agree with the boss even when a disagreement might be welcome or when the boss would easily
alter a decision if given more information. Because they
bear no relationship to the specific situation at hand,
their responses are as much an overreaction as those of
counterdependent managers. Instead of seeing the boss
as an enemy, these people deny their anger—the other
extreme—and tend to see the boss as if he or she were an
all-wise parent who should know best, should take
responsibility for their careers, train them in all they
need to know, and protect them from overly ambitious
peers.

Both counterdependence and overdependence lead
managers to hold unrealistic views of what a boss is.
Both views ignore that bosses, like everyone else, are

imperfect and fallible. They don't have unlimited time, encyclopedic knowledge, or extrasensory perception; nor are they evil enemies. They have their own pressures and concerns that are sometimes at odds with the wishes of the subordinate—and often for good reason.

Altering predispositions toward authority, especially at the extremes, is almost impossible without intensive psychotherapy (psychoanalytic theory and research suggest that such predispositions are deeply rooted in a person's personality and upbringing). However, an awareness of these extremes and the range between them can be very useful in understanding where your own predispositions fall and what the implications are for how you tend to behave in relation to your boss.

If you believe, on the one hand, that you have some tendencies toward counterdependence, you can understand and even predict what your reactions and overreactions are likely to be. If, on the other hand, you believe you have some tendencies toward overdependence, you might question the extent to which your overcompliance or inability to confront real differences may be making both you and your boss less effective.

Developing and Managing the Relationship

With a clear understanding of both your boss and yourself, you can *usually* establish a way of working together that fits both of you, that is characterized by unambiguous mutual expectations, and that helps you both be more productive and effective. The "Checklist for Managing Your Boss" summarizes some things such a relationship consists of. Following are a few more.

COMPATIBLE WORK STYLES

Above all else, a good working relationship with a boss accommodates differences in work style. For example, in one situation we studied, a manager (who had a relatively good relationship with his superior) realized that during meetings his boss would often become inattentive and sometimes brusque. The subordinate's own style tended to be discursive and exploratory. He would often digress from the topic at hand to deal with background factors, alternative approaches, and so forth. His boss preferred to discuss problems with a minimum of back-

---

Checklist for Managing Your Boss

Make Sure You Understand Your Boss and His or Her Context, Including:

• Goals and objectives

• Pressures

• Strengths, weaknesses, blind spots

• Preferred work style

Assess Yourself and Your Needs, Including:

• Strengths and weaknesses

• Personal style

• Predisposition toward dependence on authority figures

Develop and Maintain a Relationship That:

• Fits both your needs and styles

• Is characterized by mutual expectations

• Keeps your boss informed

• Is based on dependability and honesty

• Selectively uses your boss's time and resources

ground detail and became impatient and distracted whenever his subordinate digressed from the immediate issue.

Recognizing this difference in style, the manager became terser and more direct during meetings with his boss. To help himself do this, before meetings, he would develop brief agendas that he used as a guide. Whenever he felt that a digression was needed, he explained why. This small shift in his own style made these meetings more effective and far less frustrating for both of them.

Subordinates can adjust their styles in response to their bosses' preferred method for receiving information. Peter Drucker divides bosses into "listeners" and "readers." Some bosses like to get information in report form so they can read and study it. Others work better with information and reports presented in person so they can ask questions. As Drucker points out, the implications are obvious. If your boss is a listener, you brief him or her in person, *then* follow it up with a memo. If your boss is a reader, you cover important items or proposals in a memo or report, *then* discuss them.

Other adjustments can be made according to a boss's decision-making style. Some bosses prefer to be involved in decisions and problems as they arise. These are high-involvement managers who like to keep their hands on the pulse of the operation. Usually their needs (and your own) are best satisfied if you touch base with them on an ad hoc basis. A boss who has a need to be involved will become involved one way or another, so there are advantages to including him or her at your initiative. Other bosses prefer to delegate—they don't want to be involved. They expect you to come to them with major problems and inform them about any important changes.

Creating a compatible relationship also involves drawing on each other's strengths and making up for each other's weaknesses. Because he knew that the boss—the vice president of engineering—was not very good at monitoring his employees' problems, one manager we studied made a point of doing it himself. The stakes were high: The engineers and technicians were all union members, the company worked on a customer-contract basis, and the company had recently experienced a serious strike.

The manager worked closely with his boss, along with people in the scheduling department and the personnel office, to make sure that potential problems were avoided. He also developed an informal arrangement through which his boss would review with him any proposed changes in personnel or assignment policies before taking action. The boss valued his advice and credited his subordinate for improving both the performance of the division and the labor–management climate.

MUTUAL EXPECTATIONS

The subordinate who passively assumes that he or she knows what the boss expects is in for trouble. Of course, some superiors will spell out their expectations very explicitly and in great detail. But most do not. And although many corporations have systems that provide a basis for communicating expectations (such as formal planning processes, career planning reviews, and performance appraisal reviews), these systems never work perfectly. Also, between these formal reviews, expectations invariably change.

Ultimately, the burden falls on the subordinate to find out what the boss's expectations are. They can be both broad (such as what kinds of problems the boss wishes to be informed about and when) as well as very specific (such things as when a particular project should be completed and what kinds of information the boss needs in the interim).

Getting a boss who tends to be vague or not explicit to express expectations can be difficult. But effective managers find ways to get that information. Some will draft a detailed memo covering key aspects of their work and then send it to their boss for approval. They then follow this up with a face-to-face discussion in which they go over each item in the memo. A discussion like this will often surface virtually all of the boss's expectations.

Other effective managers will deal with an inexplicit boss by initiating an ongoing series of informal discussions about "good management" and "our objectives." Still others find useful information more indirectly through those who used to work for the boss and through the formal planning systems in which the boss makes commitments to his or her own superior. Which approach you choose, of course, should depend on your understanding of your boss's style.

Developing a workable set of mutual expectations also requires that you communicate your own expectations to the boss, find out if they are realistic, and influence the boss to accept the ones that are important to you. Being able to influence the boss to value your expectations can be particularly important if the boss is an overachiever. Such a boss will often set unrealistically high standards that need to be brought into line with reality.

A FLOW OF INFORMATION

How much information a boss needs about what a subordinate is doing will vary significantly depending on the boss's style, the situation he or she is in, and the confidence the boss has in the subordinate. But it is not uncommon for a boss to need more information than the subordinate would naturally supply or for the subordinate to think the boss knows more than he or she really does. Effective managers recognize that they probably underestimate what their bosses need to know and make sure they find ways to keep them informed through processes that fit their styles.

Managing the flow of information upward is particularly difficult if the boss does not like to hear about problems. Although many people would deny it, bosses often give off signals that they want to hear only good news. They show great displeasure—usually nonverbally—when someone tells them about a problem. Ignoring individual achievement, they may even evaluate more favorably subordinates who do not bring problems to them.

Nevertheless, for the good of the organization, the boss, and the subordinate, a superior needs to hear about failures as well as successes. Some subordinates deal with a good-news-only boss by finding indirect ways to get the necessary information to him or her, such as a management information system. Others see to it that potential problems, whether in the form of good surprises or bad news, are communicated immediately.

DEPENDABILITY AND HONESTY

Few things are more disabling to a boss than a subordinate on whom he cannot depend, whose work he cannot trust. Almost no one is intentionally undependable, but many managers are inadvertently so because of oversight or uncertainty about the boss's priorities. A commitment to an optimistic delivery date may please a superior in the short term but become a source of displeasure if not honored. It's difficult for a boss to rely on a subordinate who repeatedly slips deadlines. As one president (describing a subordinate) put it: "I'd rather he be more consistent even if he delivered fewer peak successes—at least I could rely on him."

Nor are many managers intentionally dishonest with their bosses. But it is easy to shade the truth and play down issues. Current concerns often become future surprise problems. It's almost impossible for bosses to work effectively if they cannot rely on a fairly accurate reading from their subordinates. Because it undermines credibility, dishonesty is perhaps the most troubling trait a subordinate can have. Without a basic level of trust, a boss feels compelled to check all of a subordinate's decisions, which makes it difficult to delegate.

GOOD USE OF TIME AND RESOURCES

Your boss is probably as limited in his or her store of time, energy, and influence as you are. Every request you make of your boss uses up some of these resources, so it's wise to draw on these resources selectively. This may sound obvious, but many managers use up their boss's time (and some of their own credibility) over relatively trivial issues.

One vice president went to great lengths to get his boss to fire a meddlesome secretary in another department. His boss had to use considerable influence to do it. Understandably, the head of the other department was not pleased. Later, when the vice president wanted to tackle more important problems, he ran into trouble. By using up blue chips on a relatively trivial issue, he had made it difficult for him and his boss to meet more important goals.

No doubt, some subordinates will resent that on top of all their other duties, they also need to take time and energy to manage their relationships with their bosses. Such managers fail to realize the importance of this activity and how it can simplify their jobs by eliminating potentially severe problems. Effective managers recognize that this part of their work is legitimate. Seeing themselves as ultimately responsible for what they achieve in an organization, they know they need to establish and manage relationships with everyone on whom they depend—and that includes the boss.

Originally published in January 2005
Reprint R0501J

Managing Oneself

PETER F. DRUCKER

Executive Summary

THROUGHOUT HISTORY, people had little need to manage their careers—they were born into their stations in life
or, in the recent past, they relied on their companies to
chart their career paths. But times have drastically
changed. Today we must all learn to manage ourselves.

What does that mean? As Peter Drucker tells us in this
seminal article first published in 1999, it means we have
to learn to develop ourselves. We have to place ourselves where we can make the greatest contribution to
our organizations and communities. And we have to stay
mentally alert and engaged during a 50-year working
life, which means knowing how and when to change the
work we do.

It may seem obvious that people achieve results by
doing what they are good at and by working in ways
that fit their abilities. But, Drucker says, very few people

actually know—let alone take advantage of—their fundamental strengths.

He challenges each of us to ask ourselves: What are
my strengths? How do I perform? What are my values?
Where do I belong? What should my contribution be?
Don't try to cage yourself, Drucker cautions. Instead, concentrate on improving the skills you have and accepting
assignments that are tailored to your individual way of
working. If you do that, you can transform yourself from
an ordinary worker into an outstanding performer.

Today's successful careers are not planned out in
advance. They develop when people are prepared for
opportunities because they have asked themselves those
questions and have rigorously assessed their unique
characteristics. This article challenges readers to take
responsibility for managing their futures, both in and out
of the office.

W E LIVE IN AN AGE OF unprecedented opportunity: If you've got ambition and smarts, you can rise to
the top of your chosen profession, regardless of where
you started out.

But with opportunity comes responsibility. Companies today aren't managing their employees' careers;
knowledge workers must, effectively, be their own chief
executive officers. It's up to you to carve out your place,
to know when to change course, and to keep yourself
engaged and productive during a work life that may span
some 50 years. To do those things well, you'll need to cultivate a deep understanding of yourself—not only what
your strengths and weaknesses are but also how you
learn, how you work with others, what your values are,

and where you can make the greatest contribution. Because only when you operate from strengths can you achieve true excellence.

History's great achievers—a Napoléon, a da Vinci, a Mozart—have always managed themselves. That, in large measure, is what makes them great achievers. But they are rare exceptions, so unusual both in their talents and their accomplishments as to be considered outside the boundaries of ordinary human existence. Now, most of us, even those of us with modest endowments, will have to learn to manage ourselves. We will have to learn to develop ourselves. We will have to place ourselves where we can make the greatest contribution. And we will have to stay mentally alert and engaged during a 50-year working life, which means knowing how and when to change the work we do.

What Are My Strengths?

Most people think they know what they are good at. They are usually wrong. More often, people know what they are not good at—and even then more people are wrong than right. And yet, a person can perform only from strength. One cannot build performance on weaknesses, let alone on something one cannot do at all.

Throughout history, people had little need to know their strengths. A person was born into a position and a line of work: The peasant's son would also be a peasant; the artisan's daughter, an artisan's wife; and so on. But now people have choices. We need to know our strengths in order to know where we belong.

The only way to discover your strengths is through feedback analysis. Whenever you make a key decision or take a key action, write down what you expect will happen. Nine or 12 months later, compare the actual results with your expectations. I have been practicing this method for 15 to 20 years now, and every time I do it, I am surprised. The feedback analysis showed me, for instance—and to my great surprise—that I have an intuitive understanding of technical people, whether they are engineers or accountants or market researchers. It also showed me that I don't really resonate with generalists.

Feedback analysis is by no means new. It was invented sometime in the fourteenth century by an otherwise totally obscure German theologian and picked up quite independently, some 150 years later, by John Calvin and Ignatius of Loyola, each of whom incorporated it into the practice of his followers. In fact, the steadfast focus on performance and results that this habit produces explains why the institutions these two men founded, the Calvinist church and the Jesuit order, came to dominate Europe within 30 years.

Practiced consistently, this simple method will show you within a fairly short period of time, maybe two or three years, where your strengths lie—and this is the most important thing to know. The method will show you what you are doing or failing to do that deprives you of the full benefits of your strengths. It will show you where you are not particularly competent. And finally, it will show you where you have no strengths and cannot perform.

Several implications for action follow from feedback analysis. First and foremost, concentrate on your strengths. Put yourself where your strengths can produce results.

Second, work on improving your strengths. Analysis will rapidly show where you need to improve skills or acquire new ones. It will also show the gaps in your knowledge—and those can usually be filled. Mathematicians are born, but everyone can learn trigonometry.

Third, discover where your intellectual arrogance is causing disabling ignorance and overcome it. Far too many people—especially people with great expertise in one area—are contemptuous of knowledge in other areas or believe that being bright is a substitute for knowledge. First-rate engineers, for instance, tend to take pride in not knowing anything about people. Human beings, they believe, are much too disorderly for the good engineering mind. Human resources professionals, by contrast, often pride themselves on their ignorance of elementary accounting or of quantitative methods altogether. But taking pride in such ignorance is self-defeating. Go to work on acquiring the skills and knowledge you need to fully realize your strengths.

It is equally essential to remedy your bad habits—the things you do or fail to do that inhibit your effectiveness and performance. Such habits will quickly show up in the feedback. For example, a planner may find that his beautiful plans fail because he does not follow through on them. Like so many brilliant people, he believes that ideas move mountains. But bulldozers move mountains; ideas show where the bulldozers should go to work. This planner will have to learn that the work does not stop when the plan is completed. He must find people to carry out the plan and explain it to them. He must adapt and change it as he puts it into action. And finally, he must decide when to stop pushing the plan.

At the same time, feedback will also reveal when the problem is a lack of manners. Manners are the lubricating oil of an organization. It is a law of nature that two moving bodies in contact with each other create friction. This is as true for human beings as it is for inanimate objects. Manners—simple things like saying "please" and "thank you" and knowing a person's name or asking after her family—enable two people to work together whether they like each other or not. Bright people, especially bright young people, often do not understand this. If analysis shows that someone's brilliant work fails again and again as soon as cooperation from others is required, it probably indicates a lack of courtesy—that is, a lack of manners.

Comparing your expectations with your results also indicates what not to do. We all have a vast number of areas in which we have no talent or skill and little chance of becoming even mediocre. In those areas a person— and especially a knowledge worker—should not take on work, jobs, and assignments. One should waste as little effort as possible on improving areas of low competence. It takes far more energy and work to improve from incompetence to mediocrity than it takes to improve from first-rate performance to excellence. And yet most people—especially most teachers and most organiza- tions—concentrate on making incompetent performers into mediocre ones. Energy, resources, and time should go instead to making a competent person into a star performer.

How Do I Perform?

Amazingly few people know how they get things done. Indeed, most of us do not even know that different peo- ple work and perform differently. Too many people work in ways that are not their ways, and that almost guaran- tees nonperformance. For knowledge workers, How do I perform? may be an even more important question than What are my strengths?

Like one's strengths, how one performs is unique. It is a matter of personality. Whether personality be a matter of nature or nurture, it surely is formed long before a person goes to work. And *how* a person performs is a given, just as *what* a person is good at or not good at is a given. A person's way of performing can be slightly modified, but it is unlikely to be completely changed—and certainly not easily. Just as people achieve results by doing what they are good at, they also achieve results by working in ways that they best perform. A few common personality traits usually determine how a person performs.

AM I A READER OR A LISTENER?

The first thing to know is whether you are a reader or a listener. Far too few people even know that there are readers and listeners and that people are rarely both. Even fewer know which of the two they themselves are. But some examples will show how damaging such ignorance can be.

When Dwight Eisenhower was Supreme Commander of the Allied forces in Europe, he was the darling of the press. His press conferences were famous for their style—General Eisenhower showed total command of whatever question he was asked, and he was able to describe a situation and explain a policy in two or three beautifully polished and elegant sentences. Ten years later, the same journalists who had been his admirers held President Eisenhower in open contempt. He never addressed the questions, they complained, but rambled on endlessly about something else. And they constantly ridiculed him for butchering the King's English in incoherent and ungrammatical answers.

Eisenhower apparently did not know that he was a reader, not a listener. When he was Supreme Commander in Europe, his aides made sure that every question from the press was presented in writing at least half an hour before a conference was to begin. And then Eisenhower was in total command. When he became president, he succeeded two listeners, Franklin D. Roosevelt and Harry Truman. Both men knew themselves to be listeners and both enjoyed free-for-all press conferences. Eisenhower may have felt that he had to do what his two predecessors had done. As a result, he never even heard the questions journalists asked. And Eisenhower is not even an extreme case of a nonlistener.

A few years later, Lyndon Johnson destroyed his presidency, in large measure, by not knowing that he was a listener. His predecessor, John Kennedy, was a reader who had assembled a brilliant group of writers as his assistants, making sure that they wrote to him before discussing their memos in person. Johnson kept these people on his staff—and they kept on writing. He never, apparently, understood one word of what they wrote. Yet as a senator, Johnson had been superb; for parliamentarians have to be, above all, listeners.

Few listeners can be made, or can make themselves, into competent readers—and vice versa. The listener who tries to be a reader will, therefore, suffer the fate of Lyndon Johnson, whereas the reader who tries to be a listener will suffer the fate of Dwight Eisenhower. They will not perform or achieve.

HOW DO I LEARN?

The second thing to know about how one performs is to know how one learns. Many first-class writers—Winston

Churchill is but one example—do poorly in school. They tend to remember their schooling as pure torture. Yet few of their classmates remember it the same way. They may not have enjoyed the school very much, but the worst they suffered was boredom. The explanation is that writers do not, as a rule, learn by listening and reading. They learn by writing. Because schools do not allow them to learn this way, they get poor grades.

Schools everywhere are organized on the assumption that there is only one right way to learn and that it is the same way for everybody. But to be forced to learn the way a school teaches is sheer hell for students who learn differently. Indeed, there are probably half a dozen different ways to learn.

There are people, like Churchill, who learn by writing. Some people learn by taking copious notes. Beethoven, for example, left behind an enormous number of sketchbooks, yet he said he never actually looked at them when he composed. Asked why he kept them, he is reported to have replied, "If I don't write it down immediately, I forget it right away. If I put it into a sketchbook, I never forget it and I never have to look it up again." Some people learn by doing. Others learn by hearing themselves talk.

A chief executive I know who converted a small and mediocre family business into the leading company in its industry was one of those people who learn by talking. He was in the habit of calling his entire senior staff into his office once a week and then talking at them for two or three hours. He would raise policy issues and argue three different positions on each one. He rarely asked his associates for comments or questions; he simply needed an audience to hear himself talk. That's how he learned. And although he is a fairly extreme case, learning through talking is by no means an unusual method.

Successful trial lawyers learn the same way, as do many medical diagnosticians (and so do I).

Of all the important pieces of self-knowledge, understanding how you learn is the easiest to acquire. When I ask people, "How do you learn?" most of them know the answer. But when I ask, "Do you act on this knowledge?" few answer yes. And yet, acting on this knowledge is the key to performance; or rather, *not* acting on this knowledge condemns one to nonperformance.

Am I a reader or a listener? and How do I learn? are the first questions to ask. But they are by no means the only ones. To manage yourself effectively, you also have to ask, Do I work well with people, or am I a loner? And if you do work well with people, you then must ask, In what relationship?

Some people work best as subordinates. General George Patton, the great American military hero of World War II, is a prime example. Patton was America's top troop commander. Yet when he was proposed for an independent command, General George Marshall, the U.S. chief of staff—and probably the most successful picker of men in U.S. history—said, "Patton is the best subordinate the American army has ever produced, but he would be the worst commander."

Some people work best as team members. Others work best alone. Some are exceptionally talented as coaches and mentors; others are simply incompetent as mentors.

Another crucial question is, Do I produce results as a decision maker or as an adviser? A great many people perform best as advisers but cannot take the burden and pressure of making the decision. A good many other people, by contrast, need an adviser to force themselves to think; then they can make decisions and act on them with speed, self-confidence, and courage.

This is a reason, by the way, that the number two person in an organization often fails when promoted to the number one position. The top spot requires a decision maker. Strong decision makers often put somebody they trust into the number two spot as their adviser—and in that position the person is outstanding. But in the number one spot, the same person fails. He or she knows what the decision should be but cannot accept the responsibility of actually making it.

Other important questions to ask include, Do I perform well under stress, or do I need a highly structured and predictable environment? Do I work best in a big organization or a small one? Few people work well in all kinds of environments. Again and again, I have seen people who were very successful in large organizations flounder miserably when they moved into smaller ones. And the reverse is equally true.

The conclusion bears repeating: Do not try to change yourself—you are unlikely to succeed. But work hard to improve the way you perform. And try not to take on work you cannot perform or will only perform poorly.

What Are My Values?

To be able to manage yourself, you finally have to ask, What are my values? This is not a question of ethics. With respect to ethics, the rules are the same for everybody, and the test is a simple one. I call it the "mirror test."

In the early years of this century, the most highly respected diplomat of all the great powers was the

German ambassador in London. He was clearly destined for great things—to become his country's foreign minister, at least, if not its federal chancellor. Yet in 1906 he abruptly resigned rather than preside over a dinner given by the diplomatic corps for Edward VII. The king was a notorious womanizer and made it clear what kind of dinner he wanted. The ambassador is reported to have said, "I refuse to see a pimp in the mirror in the morning when I shave."

That is the mirror test. Ethics requires that you ask yourself, What kind of person do I want to see in the mirror in the morning? What is ethical behavior in one kind of organization or situation is ethical behavior in another. But ethics is only part of a value system—especially of an organization's value system.

To work in an organization whose value system is unacceptable or incompatible with one's own condemns a person both to frustration and to nonperformance.

Consider the experience of a highly successful human resources executive whose company was acquired by a bigger organization. After the acquisition, she was promoted to do the kind of work she did best, which included selecting people for important positions. The executive deeply believed that a company should hire people for such positions from the outside only after exhausting all the inside possibilities. But her new company believed in first looking outside "to bring in fresh blood." There is something to be said for both approaches—in my experience, the proper one is to do some of both. They are, however, fundamentally incompatible—not as policies but as values. They bespeak different views of the relationship between organizations and people; different views of the responsibility of an organization to its people and their development; and different views of a person's most important contribution to an enterprise. After several years of frustration, the executive quit—at considerable financial loss. Her values and the values of the organization simply were not compatible.

Similarly, whether a pharmaceutical company tries to obtain results by making constant, small improvements or by achieving occasional, highly expensive, and risky "breakthroughs" is not primarily an economic question. The results of either strategy may be pretty much the same. At bottom, there is a conflict between a value system that sees the company's contribution in terms of helping physicians do better what they already do and a value system that is oriented toward making scientific discoveries.

Whether a business should be run for short-term results or with a focus on the long term is likewise a question of values. Financial analysts believe that businesses can be run for both simultaneously. Successful businesspeople know better. To be sure, every company has to produce short-term results. But in any conflict between short-term results and long-term growth, each company will determine its own priority. This is not primarily a disagreement about economics. It is fundamentally a value conflict regarding the function of a business and the responsibility of management.

Value conflicts are not limited to business organizations. One of the fastest-growing pastoral churches in the United States measures success by the number of new parishioners. Its leadership believes that what matters is how many newcomers join the congregation. The Good Lord will then minister to their spiritual needs or at least to the needs of a sufficient percentage. Another pastoral, evangelical church believes that what matters is people's spiritual growth. The church eases out newcomers who join but do not enter into its spiritual life.

Again, this is not a matter of numbers. At first glance, it appears that the second church grows more slowly. But it retains a far larger proportion of newcomers than the first one does. Its growth, in other words, is more solid. This is also not a theological problem, or only secondarily so. It is a problem about values. In a public debate, one pastor argued, "Unless you first come to church, you will never find the gate to the Kingdom of Heaven."

"No," answered the other. "Until you first look for the gate to the Kingdom of Heaven, you don't belong in church."

Organizations, like people, have values. To be effective in an organization, a person's values must be compatible with the organization's values. They do not need to be the same, but they must be close enough to coexist. Otherwise, the person will not only be frustrated but also will not produce results.

A person's strengths and the way that person performs rarely conflict; the two are complementary. But there is sometimes a conflict between a person's values and his or her strengths. What one does well—even very well and successfully—may not fit with one's value system. In that case, the work may not appear to be worth devoting one's life to (or even a substantial portion thereof).

If I may, allow me to interject a personal note. Many years ago, I too had to decide between my values and what I was doing successfully. I was doing very well as a young investment banker in London in the mid-1930s, and the work clearly fit my strengths. Yet I did not see myself making a contribution as an asset manager.

People, I realized, were what I valued, and I saw no point in being the richest man in the cemetery. I had no money and no other job prospects. Despite the continuing Depression, I quit—and it was the right thing to do. Values, in other words, are and should be the ultimate test.

Where Do I Belong?

A small number of people know very early where they belong. Mathematicians, musicians, and cooks, for instance, are usually mathematicians, musicians, and cooks by the time they are four or five years old. Physicians usually decide on their careers in their teens, if not earlier. But most people, especially highly gifted people, do not really know where they belong until they are well past their mid-twenties. By that time, however, they should know the answers to the three questions: What are my strengths? How do I perform? and, What are my values? And then they can and should decide where they belong.

Or rather, they should be able to decide where they do *not* belong. The person who has learned that he or she does not perform well in a big organization should have learned to say no to a position in one. The person who has learned that he or she is not a decision maker should have learned to say no to a decision-making assignment. A General Patton (who probably never learned this himself) should have learned to say no to an independent command.

Equally important, knowing the answer to these questions enables a person to say to an opportunity, an offer, or an assignment, "Yes, I will do that. But this is the way I should be doing it. This is the way it should be structured. This is the way the relationships should be. These are the kind of results you should expect from me, and in this time frame, because this is who I am."

Successful careers are not planned. They develop when people are prepared for opportunities because they know their strengths, their method of work, and their values. Knowing where one belongs can transform an ordinary person—hardworking and competent but otherwise mediocre—into an outstanding performer.

What Should I Contribute?

Throughout history, the great majority of people never had to ask the question, What should I contribute? They were told what to contribute, and their tasks were dictated either by the work itself—as it was for the peasant or artisan—or by a master or a mistress—as it was for domestic servants. And until very recently, it was taken for granted that most people were subordinates who did as they were told. Even in the 1950s and 1960s, the new knowledge workers (the so-called organization men) looked to their company's personnel department to plan their careers.

Then in the late 1960s, no one wanted to be told what to do any longer. Young men and women began to ask, What do *I* want to do? And what they heard was that the way to contribute was to "do your own thing." But this solution was as wrong as the organization men's had been. Very few of the people who believed that doing one's own thing would lead to contribution, self-fulfillment, and success achieved any of the three.

But still, there is no return to the old answer of doing what you are told or assigned to do. Knowledge workers in particular have to learn to ask a question

that has not been asked before: What *should* my contribution be? To answer it, they must address three distinct elements: What does the situation require? Given
my strengths, my way of performing, and my values,
how can I make the greatest contribution to what
needs to be done? And finally, What results have to be
achieved to make a difference?

Consider the experience of a newly appointed hospital
administrator. The hospital was big and prestigious, but it
had been coasting on its reputation for 30 years. The new
administrator decided that his contribution should be to
establish a standard of excellence in one important area
within two years. He chose to focus on the emergency
room, which was big, visible, and sloppy. He decided that
every patient who came into the ER had to be seen by a
qualified nurse within 60 seconds. Within 12 months, the
hospital's emergency room had become a model for all
hospitals in the United States, and within another two
years, the whole hospital had been transformed.

As this example suggests, it is rarely possible—or even
particularly fruitful—to look too far ahead. A plan can
usually cover no more than 18 months and still be reasonably clear and specific. So the question in most cases
should be, Where and how can I achieve results that will
make a difference within the next year and a half? The
answer must balance several things. First, the results
should be hard to achieve—they should require "stretch-
ing," to use the current buzzword. But also, they should
be within reach. To aim at results that cannot be
achieved—or that can be only under the most unlikely
circumstances—is not being ambitious; it is being fool-
ish. Second, the results should be meaningful. They
should make a difference. Finally, results should be visible and, if at all possible, measurable. From this will

come a course of action: what to do, where and how to start, and what goals and deadlines to set.

Responsibility for Relationships

Very few people work by themselves and achieve results by themselves—a few great artists, a few great scientists, a few great athletes. Most people work with others and are effective with other people. That is true whether they are members of an organization or independently employed. Managing yourself requires taking responsibility for relationships. This has two parts.

The first is to accept the fact that other people are as much individuals as you yourself are. They perversely insist on behaving like human beings. This means that they too have their strengths; they too have their ways of getting things done; they too have their values. To be effective, therefore, you have to know the strengths, the performance modes, and the values of your coworkers.

That sounds obvious, but few people pay attention to it. Typical is the person who was trained to write reports in his or her first assignment because that boss was a reader. Even if the next boss is a listener, the person goes on writing reports that, invariably, produce no results. Invariably the boss will think the employee is stupid, incompetent, and lazy, and he or she will fail. But that could have been avoided if the employee had only looked at the new boss and analyzed how *this* boss performs.

Bosses are neither a title on the organization chart nor a "function." They are individuals and are entitled to do their work in the way they do it best. It is incumbent on the people who work with them to observe them, to find out how they work, and to adapt themselves to what makes their bosses most effective. This, in fact, is the secret of "managing" the boss.

The same holds true for all your coworkers. Each works his or her way, not your way. And each is entitled to work in his or her way. What matters is whether they perform and what their values are. As for how they perform—each is likely to do it differently. The first secret of effectiveness is to understand the people you work with and depend on so that you can make use of their strengths, their ways of working, and their values. Working relationships are as much based on the people as they are on the work.

The second part of relationship responsibility is taking responsibility for communication. Whenever I, or any other consultant, start to work with an organization, the first thing I hear about are all the personality conflicts. Most of these arise from the fact that people do not know what other people are doing and how they do their work, or what contribution the other people are concentrating on and what results they expect. And the reason they do not know is that they have not asked and therefore have not been told.

This failure to ask reflects human stupidity less than it reflects human history. Until recently, it was unnecessary to tell any of these things to anybody. In the medieval city, everyone in a district plied the same trade. In the countryside, everyone in a valley planted the same crop as soon as the frost was out of the ground. Even those few people who did things that were not "common" worked alone, so they did not have to tell anyone what they were doing.

Today the great majority of people work with others who have different tasks and responsibilities. The marketing vice president may have come out of sales and know everything about sales, but she knows nothing about the things she has never done—pricing, advertising, packaging, and the like. So the people who do these things must make sure that the marketing vice president understands what they are trying to do, why they are trying to do it, how they are going to do it, and what results to expect.

If the marketing vice president does not understand what these high-grade knowledge specialists are doing, it is primarily their fault, not hers. They have not educated her. Conversely, it is the marketing vice president's responsibility to make sure that all of her coworkers understand how she looks at marketing: what her goals are, how she works, and what she expects of herself and of each one of them.

Even people who understand the importance of taking responsibility for relationships often do not communicate sufficiently with their associates. They are afraid of being thought presumptuous or inquisitive or stupid. They are wrong. Whenever someone goes to his or her associates and says, "This is what I am good at. This is how I work. These are my values. This is the contribution I plan to concentrate on and the results I should be expected to deliver," the response is always, "This is most helpful. But why didn't you tell me earlier?"

And one gets the same reaction—without exception, in my experience—if one continues by asking, "And what do I need to know about your strengths, how you perform, your values, and your proposed contribution?" In fact, knowledge workers should request this of everyone with whom they work, whether as subordinate, superior, colleague, or team member. And again, whenever this is done, the reaction is always, "Thanks for asking me. But why didn't you ask me earlier?"

Organizations are no longer built on force but on trust. The existence of trust between people does not necessarily mean that they like one another. It means that they understand one another. Taking responsibility for relationships is therefore an absolute necessity. It is a duty. Whether one is a member of the organization, a consultant to it, a supplier, or a distributor, one owes that responsibility to all one's coworkers: those whose work one depends on as well as those who depend on one's own work.

The Second Half of Your Life

When work for most people meant manual labor, there was no need to worry about the second half of your life. You simply kept on doing what you had always done. And if you were lucky enough to survive 40 years of hard work in the mill or on the railroad, you were quite happy to spend the rest of your life doing nothing. Today, however, most work is knowledge work, and knowledge workers are not "finished" after 40 years on the job, they are merely bored.

We hear a great deal of talk about the midlife crisis of the executive. It is mostly boredom. At 45, most executives have reached the peak of their business careers, and they know it. After 20 years of doing very much the same kind of work, they are very good at their jobs. But they are not learning or contributing or deriving challenge and satisfaction from the job. And yet they are still likely to face another 20 if not 25 years of work. That is why managing oneself increasingly leads one to begin a second career.

There are three ways to develop a second career. The first is actually to start one. Often this takes nothing more than moving from one kind of organization to another: the divisional controller in a large corporation, for instance, becomes the controller of a medium-sized hospital. But there are also growing numbers of people who move into different lines of work altogether: the business executive or government official who enters the ministry at 45, for instance; or the midlevel manager who leaves corporate life after 20 years to attend law school and become a small-town attorney.

We will see many more second careers undertaken by people who have achieved modest success in their first jobs. Such people have substantial skills, and they know how to work. They need a community—the house is empty with the children gone—and they need income as well. But above all, they need challenge.

The second way to prepare for the second half of your life is to develop a parallel career. Many people who are very successful in their first careers stay in the work they have been doing, either on a full-time or part-time or consulting basis. But in addition, they create a parallel job, usually in a nonprofit organization, that takes another ten hours of work a week. They might take over the administration of their church, for instance, or the presidency of the local Girl Scouts council. They might run the battered women's shelter, work as a children's librarian for the local public library, sit on the school board, and so on.

Finally, there are the social entrepreneurs. These are usually people who have been very successful in their first careers. They love their work, but it no longer challenges them. In many cases they keep on doing what they have been doing all along but spend less and less of their time on it. They also start another activity, usually a nonprofit. My friend Bob Buford, for example, built a very successful television company that he still runs. But he has also founded and built a successful nonprofit organization that works with Protestant churches, and he is building another to teach social entrepreneurs how to manage their own nonprofit ventures while still running their original businesses.

People who manage the second half of their lives may always be a minority. The majority may "retire on the job" and count the years until their actual retirement. But it is this minority, the men and women who see a long working-life expectancy as an opportunity both for themselves and for society, who will become leaders and models.

There is one prerequisite for managing the second half of your life: You must begin long before you enter it. When it first became clear 30 years ago that working-life expectancies were lengthening very fast, many observers (including myself) believed that retired people would increasingly become volunteers for nonprofit institutions. That has not happened. If one does not begin to volunteer before one is 40 or so, one will not volunteer once past 60.

Similarly, all the social entrepreneurs I know began to work in their chosen second enterprise long before they reached their peak in their original business. Consider the example of a successful lawyer, the legal counsel to a large corporation, who has started a venture to establish model schools in his state. He began to do volunteer legal work for the schools when he was around 35. He was elected to the school board at age 40. At age 50, when he had amassed a fortune, he started his own enterprise to build and to run model schools. He is, however, still working nearly full-time as the lead counsel in the company he helped found as a young lawyer.

There is another reason to develop a second major interest, and to develop it early. No one can expect to live very long without experiencing a serious setback in his or her life or work. There is the competent engineer who is passed over for promotion at age 45. There is the competent college professor who realizes at age 42 that she will never get a professorship at a big university, even though she may be fully qualified for it. There are tragedies in one's family life: the breakup of one's marriage or the loss of a child. At such times, a second major interest—not just a hobby—may make all the difference. The engineer, for example, now knows that he has not been very successful in his job. But in his outside activity—as church treasurer, for example—he is a success. One's family may break up, but in that outside activity there is still a community.

In a society in which success has become so terribly important, having options will become increasingly vital. Historically, there was no such thing as "success." The overwhelming majority of people did not expect anything but to stay in their "proper station," as an old English prayer has it. The only mobility was downward mobility.

In a knowledge society, however, we expect everyone to be a success. This is clearly an impossibility. For a great many people, there is at best an absence of failure. Wherever there is success, there has to be failure. And then it is vitally important for the individual, and equally for the individual's family, to have an area in which he or she can contribute, make a difference, and be *somebody*. That means finding a second area—whether in a second career, a parallel career, or a social venture—that offers an opportunity for being a leader, for being respected, for being a success.

The challenges of managing oneself may seem obvious, if not elementary. And the answers may seem self-evident to the point of appearing naïve. But managing oneself requires new and unprecedented things from the individual, and especially from the knowledge worker. In effect, managing oneself demands that each knowledge worker think and behave like a chief executive officer. Further, the shift from manual workers who do as they are told to knowledge workers who have to manage themselves profoundly challenges social structure. Every existing society, even the most individualistic one, takes two things for granted, if only subconsciously: that organizations outlive workers, and that most people stay put.

But today the opposite is true. Knowledge workers outlive organizations, and they are mobile. The need to manage oneself is therefore creating a revolution in human affairs.

Originally published in January 2005
Reprint R0501K

About the Contributors

BRIANNA BARKER is a PhD candidate at the University of Michigan.

DAN CIAMPA is an adviser to senior executives and coauthor of *Right from the Start: Taking Charge in a New Leadership Role.*

PETER F. DRUCKER is the Marie Rankin Clarke Professor of Social Science and Management (emeritus) at Claremont Graduate University.

JANE DUTTON is professor at the Stephen M. Ross School of Business at the University of Michigan.

JOHN J. GABARRO is the UPS Foundation Professor of Human Resource Management at Harvard Business School

EDWARD M. HALLOWELL is a psychiatrist, founder of the Hallowell Center for Cognitive and Emotional Health, and author of *Driven to Distraction.*

EMILY HEAPHY is a PhD candidate at the Stephen M. Ross School of Business at the University of Michigan.

DOMINIC HOULDER is the associate dean of the Sloan Fellowship program at London Business School.

HERMINIA IBARRA is the Insead Chaired Professor of Organizational Behavior at Insead.

JOHN P. KOTTER was the Konosuke Matushita Professor of Leadership at Harvard Business School.

KENT LINEBACK is a writer and coach on storytelling and change, based in Cambridge, MA.

ROBERT QUINN is professor at the Stephen M. Ross School of Business at the University of Michigan.

LAURA MORGAN ROBERTS is an assistant professor of organizational behavior at Harvard Business School.

GRETCHEN SPREITZER is a professor at the Stephen M. Ross School of Business at the University of Michigan.

DONALD N. SULL is an associate professor of management practice at London Business School.

DAISY WADEMAN is author of *Remember Who You Are: Life Stories That Inspire the Heart and Mind.*

Index